W9-DHG-280

INTENSE MINDS

Through the Eyes of Young People with Bipolar Disorder

By Tracy Anglada

Note for Librarians: A cataloguing record for this book is available from Library and Archives Canada at www.collectionscanada.ca/amicus/index-e.html
ISBN 1-4251-6701-2

Printed on paper with minimum 30% recycled fibre.
Trafford's print shop runs on "green energy" from solar, wind and other environmentally-friendly power sources.

TRAFFORD PUBLISHING™
Offices in Canada, USA, Ireland and UK

Book sales for North America and international:
Trafford Publishing, 6E–2333 Government St.,
Victoria, BC V8T 4P4 CANADA
phone 250 383 6864 (toll-free 1 888 232 4444)
fax 250 383 6804; email to orders@trafford.com
Book sales in Europe:
Trafford Publishing (UK) Limited, 9 Park End Street, 2nd Floor
Oxford, UK OX1 1HH UNITED KINGDOM
phone 44 (0)1865 722 113 (local rate 0845 230 9601)
facsimile 44 (0)1865 722 868; info.uk@trafford.com
Order online at:
trafford.com/06-0723

10 9 8 7 6 5 4 3 2

Acknowledgment

A number of courageous people came forward to share their intimate thoughts and feelings with me, making this book possible. Some of these courageous individuals are children diagnosed with bipolar disorder. The majority are adults diagnosed with the illness, whose symptom onset began in childhood. This is a unique group of people who know firsthand what it is like to grow up with bipolar disorder. I wish to thank each of them, not only for their insight, but for their will to survive and, through that survival, to enlighten others. In order to protect the anonymity of the participants, some names have been changed.

I would also like to acknowledge the encouragement of others along the way. I thank my husband for his loving support, and for putting up with a distracted wife so that I could accomplish this project. Thank you to my children, who are forever my inspiration. Thank you to my mother, who gave me the gift of words. Thank you to my father, who helped me to widen my vision. Thank you to Carolyn, for her gentle prodding and realistic help with setting goals. Thank you to Todd, for his encouragement and for having the insight to keep his artwork and poetry from his days as a youth with bipolar disorder. Thank you to Dawn, for collaborating on new artwork and poetry. Also, thank you to the numerous people who critiqued various versions of my manuscript.

Thank you to both Andrew Randall and Bryna Hebert for their proofreading assistance and technical expertise.

Lastly, I must acknowledge the limitations of this work. Bipolar disorder has been called a chameleon. It can look very different in different people. Rory, one of my courageous participants, put it very well: "Not everybody with bipolar is the same. They all struggle with different issues." Even so, there is a shared experience. The same feelings were expressed over and over by those participating in this project. These participants were sometimes surprised to learn that others felt the same way. This book will share with you the common themes and feelings expressed by those who grew up with bipolar disorder.

It is my wish that as you read the pages of this book, you will become committed to helping children who suffer from this illness. I also wish for healing and peace to those of my adult readers who were once these very children.

"We can't look back to change the past.
We can't look back to mourn.
We can't look back to give excuse
But we must look back to learn and understand our pain."

Todd Schwarz

Table of Contents

SECTION 1 - DEPRESSION

Darkness Within

SECTION 2 - MANIA

Riding the Wave

SECTION 3 - WORLDS COLLIDE

The Wind Changes

SECTION 4 - LIVING

Survival

SECTION 5 - MAKING A DIFFERENCE

Plea for Help

An Introduction

I remember the first time I heard about bipolar disorder. At 17 years of age, the term meant little to me. More than a decade later, my son was diagnosed with the condition. All of a sudden, the term took on a whole new importance. Was it not important before? Of course it was important. But, like so many people before me, I did not grasp its importance until my life was touched in a very personal way. I began reading and researching with an insatiable appetite. I learned much about what was then a very new diagnosis in children. Bipolar disorder is a cyclical illness with extreme "ups" or manias, alternating with extreme "downs" or depressions. Each of these phases comes with its own collection of symptoms. Most young people with the condition cycle rapidly, having many bouts of depression and mania in very short periods of time. I learned that the illness presents itself differently, with much more chronic irritability, in children as compared to adults. These children spend much time in a "mixed" state, exhibiting symptoms of both depression and mania together. As I grew in my understanding, I gained a whole new vocabulary, and a whole new perspective. Still, something was missing.

I witnessed the suffering of my own child, who conveyed to me as best he could the intense feelings he was experiencing. I read symptom list after symptom list. They seemed to laugh at me from their cozy places on the typewritten page. How could these feelings, wreaking so much havoc and chaos on those afflicted, be contained in a list? Lists of symptoms are important to understanding bipolar disorder. Doctors use them to make diagnoses and record symptoms. Parents use them to keep track of their child's mood states. However, a person could easily read a list of symptoms yet not comprehend the depth of their meaning or the effect they have on a growing child. How can we truly understand the intensity of the suffering experienced by children with bipolar disorder? It takes more than could ever be conveyed in a list. It takes more than medical textbooks and a clinical evaluation. It takes attentiveness, empathy and compassion. It takes opening up one's mind and heart to the experiences of others.

Why? Why should we stretch ourselves to see as others see? It's not particularly comfortable. In fact, it can be quite scary. It's much easier to stay blinded to everything outside of our personal reality. Those of us who stretch the limits of our comfort zone by embracing the experience of others will be enriched. More than personal enrichment, we will be in a much better position to understand young people who suffer from bipolar disorder and help them grow into the healthy, productive adults they deserve to be.

Even for those who long to have it, acquiring such

insight is no easy task. It's not always easy for children to express themselves. It can be hard for them to convey what they feel. It can be even harder for us to listen, truly listen, and understand. When my son started expressing his scary feelings to me, my first reaction was to negate his feelings. I didn't do it on purpose; nevertheless, I did it. So when he said, "I want the neighbors' dog to bite me!" my response was, "No, you don't. That would hurt." When he would tell me about a particularly graphic dream, I would stop him and tell him not to talk about such things. When he expressed excitement at the thought of no longer being alive, I could not believe that he really felt that way. I heard, but I didn't listen. Perhaps I thought if I denied the existence of such feelings, then they wouldn't be real. How could I accept that my 6-year-old wanted to be hurt? The idea that my child could have

such pain inside was devastating to me. His experience was so far away from my own that I could not comprehend it. My assumption was that my children would experience childhood as I had. The growing reality was far from the beauty I remembered as a child, yet I began to listen and believe my

son. I also validated and accepted his feelings. Still, I knew that I was a long way from truly understanding them. Was it possible to gain such understanding? If so, how could I share that knowledge with others?

I found such understanding by listening to children with bipolar disorder, and by listening to adults whose symptoms emerged during childhood. These are the ones who truly know what it feels like to grow up with bipolar disorder. This book is the culmination of their shared experiences and thoughts. Wherever possible, I let them speak directly to you, the reader, so that you too may listen and understand.

I don't expect you to be comfortable through your entire reading of this book. The intense feelings and experiences, so candidly expressed by those interviewed and recorded within these pages, can be overwhelming and emotionally taxing. Bipolar disorder is not a comfortable experience. Some of the material presented here is difficult to accept. But turning away is equivalent to saying, "No, you don't feel that way." We can't negate these experiences. We must listen and stretch our minds to learn. Those who shared their experiences with me had to step out of their comfort zone and bravely bare some very intimate feelings. Some had never told another soul what they shared with me for this book, which is why their identities remain disguised. Any similarity in experience to someone with the same name is purely coincidental. For some of these courageous people, this project brought up difficult memories and hurtful feelings. They struggled to share these for your benefit, and that of future generations. No child should suffer such pain. By understanding, we can make a difference and touch the lives of young people with bipolar disorder.

SECTION 1

Depression

"It lays there still, broken, in agony, in pain,
With a scattered meaningless semblance
Of its once courageous luster."

Todd Schwarz

Darkness Within

A broad smile spread across my son's face. His eyes shone brightly and he turned to me to share his good news. What was the cause of excitement for my 6-year-old son? We were at a meeting, and the speaker was describing the horrible plight of the Biblical man Job.

"Job was so sick, he wanted to die," said the speaker.

What was my son's good news in response to that statement? Two simple words: "Like me!" He had finally found someone he could relate to, someone else who wanted to die. It was comforting for him to know that he was not alone. It was no comfort to me. As a parent, those were the worst words I could have heard.

What could a child be experiencing that makes death seem to be a welcome relief? In the case above, it was the depressive phase of bipolar disorder. Of all the mood states relating to bipolar disorder in children, it is the depression that seems indelibly burned into their very existence, causing painful memories and scars that last a lifetime. For some children experiencing this phase of the illness, the feelings we will discuss are a mixed-up web of emotions that can't be untangled one from another. For others, it is a progression from one feeling to the next, leaving hope that someone will step in and halt that progression for young people now and for future generations.

> "I felt sad inwardly most of the time. I felt a darkness within that never went away." *Marty*

1st thing • Always a deep sadness.

Empty Inside

What do you feel inside? When everything is quiet and you close your eyes, what is it that fills your soul? Is it peaceful? Is it a warm contentment? Not if you are a child with bipolar disorder. There is something distinct that wells up and fills that inner space. It is emptiness; a huge, empty expanse of nothingness.

Avoiding–not enjoying sleep.

"I felt like the emptiness in me was going to swallow me whole, and I didn't know where to go for help. Each day became progressively worse." *Drew*

"It was confusing because I was not really feeling anything at all. I was empty, yet I was hurting. There was not a reason for me to hurt, but I did, and I hurt inside bad! I used to pray to God to give me a small hole that I could crawl into in my room. I wanted to crawl into this small hole, shut the door and lock it, and curl up in a ball and die. There were times I would think that this emptiness was so vast that it would never go away, and that I wanted death. I would think about killing myself, and what would happen as a result. It was a very confusing time." *Grace*

"I felt numb. I would not listen to my music. Every time my depression lifted, I listened to my music again." *Abbey*

"I felt 'empty' often. I remember the dark days well. I remember crying in a corner on my birthday, wishing I hadn't even woken up at all – ever. I was 15. I was often suicidal. I can't remember enjoying anything besides music. I felt I was in a very, very, deep, dark hole all alone. I would look at other kids and wonder how they did it, or why they did it: played and laughed. Sometimes I thought they were stupid, other times I felt sad that I couldn't do it also. The times I would play, right in the middle of a game I would find myself feeling stupid, stop, and go back to my hole to wonder how they did it. I never enjoyed life in general. I remember praying in my childlike terms, 'Have my brain explode,' so I didn't have to wake up and do it all over again and feel the way I had felt the days or weeks before." *Lee*

"I remember thinking, 'I am never happy.' I had a good life and a lot of things many kids didn't have – horses, trips, etc. I was not ungrateful, but just never felt like I could be happy. I don't remember liking much of anything. I thought that I just was a sad person and would always be one." *Jill*

Even happy occasions are totally overshadowed or overwhelmed by this "empty" feeling. Sometimes, children can mask over this feeling temporarily and put on a happy face for others. But the inner feeling remains. Other times, the empty feeling may retreat for a while, only to resurface and overtake the memory of the happy occasion. This is a difficult concept for many adults to understand. If it appears that a child is experiencing happiness, it is hard to believe that the child is depressed. Afterward, the child may deny having experienced any happiness to begin with, leaving loved ones confused. Thus, despite a parent's efforts to outline happy experiences, the child may deny ever being happy. Many children with bipolar disorder have trouble identifying feelings that are outside of their current mood state. When my own son was questioned about this, he assured me that even when he was happy on the outside, he was sad on the inside.

Crying

Babies cry to express a need that cannot yet be verbalized. Older children and adults cry to express pain or sorrow. Even intense joy can be expressed through tears. It is not surprising, then, that many children who experience the intense emotions of bipolar disorder cry a lot. At times, the crying is a direct expression of the inner pain. Other times, it is a plea for relief. Either way, it is heartbreaking.

"I remember at about age 9 sitting in my windowsill upstairs late at night, staring out the window crying, sobbing. Crying out to God for help, not knowing at the time why or what was wrong with me, just feeling alone, outside, rejected and having nowhere to turn, having a feeling of impending doom. I often felt I didn't want to be on this Earth." *Erin*

"From about 11 years old on, I felt so empty and couldn't understand why. I would go in my room and just cry for hours for no reason at all. I remember wandering around after school just feeling like something was wrong, but not knowing what it was." *Carmen*

"I would sit there (in a closet) for hours in the dark. At first I did a lot of crying, but then later, I felt like I was hurting too badly to cry. I would sit there and talk to God and beg him to take me to heaven." *Dale*

"I'd end up in tears in the restaurant, and I, as a young kid, would ask for my Mom's car keys so I could go sit in the car and scream and cry. I felt crazy and hopeless and wished someone understood me. I would always stay in the car hungry, and no one would come to get me." *Jordan*

"No one ever understood why I cried so much, because they were all very kind to me. I felt alone and sad always. I knew that I was not the same as everyone else. My mother would hold me and talk to me and tell me how much she loved me. She seemed to understand better than anyone what I was feeling. Everyone else, I felt, just got annoyed with me because I was such a crybaby." *Alex*

"Tears always streamed down my face when I was depressed, and

I often couldn't express my pain and agony." *Miranda*

For some young people with bipolar disorder, the tears are just waiting to overflow, but they need another reason to get started. Thus, very small things become a release to express the inner pain. A small trigger then will bring on a response totally out of proportion. The response can't be explained by the child, because there are no words for their feelings, only tears.

> "I remember many times feeling very sad for no reason. Once, I stepped on an ant because he was in my driveway. Then I cried for nearly three hours. My parents did not know what was wrong. I was sad because the ant no longer had life, and I had ended that life." *Grace*

> "I feel very sad when I don't think I have any friends, because no one will play with me. Then I think everyone hates me, and it makes me cry for a long time. I wish adults knew that I wish they could make the sadness go away." *Alisha, age 7*

> "Once, we went to Epcot. You can imagine how excited I was. I especially wanted to see the Universe of Energy, the Dinosaurs. I had my camera ready and could barely stand still during the 45-minute wait, and through the introduction movie. Well, something went wrong with my camera, the flash didn't work. I panicked and tried to get it to work, but it wouldn't. I got tunnel vision and was absolutely crushed. After the ride, I just sat on a bench and cried. There was no consoling me. I didn't enjoy anything the rest of the day because of it." *Todd*

> "Random things set me off crying uncontrollably, unable to stop. Why did I feel so sad about insignificant events? Why did I feel so sad? When I was 7 or 8 years old, my friend and I had entered

the school art contest. On the day the pictures were judged, they were all hung up in the hallways. My picture was next to my friend's and I had a blue ribbon for first prize. She had an honorable mention. This made me so sad, and I couldn't understand why. Before I knew it, I was crying uncontrollably. It felt out of my control. I could just keep crying and crying and use up all my strength. I always cried until I fell asleep from exhaustion, or until my sobbing made me cough and dry heave. My body would take over after crying for so long and I would collapse on my bed until I fell asleep." *Rory*

Irritation

Dealing with a child who is crying may engender some feelings of compassion or sympathy. Dealing with an irritable child will not! Yet, irritation, in the physical sense of the word, can be the body's indication that something is wrong. For example, if you have an "irritation" on your skin, it becomes red, inflamed and ultra sensitive to outside stimuli, alerting you that something is wrong. Imagine you have an open wound that has become infected. Your skin is "irritated," and rightly so, as it deals with an uncomfortable physical condition. Doing everyday normal tasks adds to this discomfort and irritation. Putting on your clothes is now uncomfortable. Walking now hurts. A person inadvertently brushes against your wound, causing further discomfort. Prior to having this irritation, these everyday activities were not problematic.

Now, you likely avoid certain things to prevent further irritation. But you also know that, with care, this irritation will subside, allowing you to resume your normal activities.

Irritability in bipolar disorder is no less a physical response. It is a symptom of both depression and mania. Children with bipolar disorder frequently have chronic irritability. Perhaps you are someone who has lived with an irritable person. If so, you know that it is extremely difficult. Imagine being the child whose illness causes him to be irritable. Now consider that the child's physical irritation becomes sensitive to everyday normal activities, causing further irritation. This interferes with friendships and encourages the child to seek refuge from situations in order to find relief from the irritation. Just like other physical conditions, it requires healing in order for the irritation to go away.

> "By the time I was six, I was exhibiting daily irritability. My clothes didn't feel right, my hair was too tight, etc. I tortured my mother daily because no matter how or what she did to help, it wouldn't suit. It was a war of wills, because she had preconceived ideas of how I should look and dress." *Gina*

> "I remember feeling irritable. Having people around me annoyed me and made it worse. Everything was like nails on a chalkboard. I had to have things certain ways in order to not be irritated, so it was easier to be alone. It was worse in adolescence. I was depressive and found everything to be serious. I was very intense and loved to listen to very mellow, sad, depressive music." *Austin*

"A lot of my problems were with irritability." *Todd*

"All of my friends annoy me!" *Savannah, age 14*

"When I first began to feel depressed, I felt mostly numb and irritable. I felt alone and worthless, as if life had no meaning. I couldn't understand why I was different, and I knew that there was something wrong with me, but didn't know what." *Drew*

"I recall feeling extremely irritable. If a fellow student, a parent or my sister looked at me the wrong way, I would wish they would die." *Grace*

Pain

Along with the emptiness and irritation noted above, comes pain, real pain. It's easy for us to understand the pain that comes with a broken bone or a burn because we can associate the effect with a cause. If we see our child fall off a bike and hear his cries, we can empathize with his pain. As a parent, we will likely come running to the rescue. Or, if our child touches a hot stove, we will immediately understand that the burn is painful. We can also see the physical evidence, perhaps a bruise or blistered skin. But how does one understand internal anguish and the resulting pain it causes?

If there is a traumatic experience then it becomes a little easier to understand. People who are mourning the death of a loved one feel pain. It's accepted that their anguish is real, because it is associated with a reason. What of children who exhibit symptoms of bipolar disorder as young as in their preschool years, without any apparent outside trigger? What causes them to feel pain?

The key to understanding this pain is to realize that bipolar disorder itself is the cause. It's an illness that causes pain … and more than emotional pain. It can also cause stomach aches, back aches, muscle aches and headaches. Just as these types of pains are real, so too is the emotional pain.

> "I felt like some kind of freak and very self-conscious all the time. Not one person even seemed to notice the change in me, or the pain and daily struggle I was having." *Bobbi*

It is not always easy to identify these feelings in children. I can vividly remember sitting with my own son at his doctor's appointment. After reviewing family history and current symptoms, the doctor asked my son if he ever had thoughts of hurting himself. I remember shaking my head "no" to the doctor. When I looked over at my son, he was nodding his head "yes." If we don't know the questions to ask, we may not gain the information we need.

Fortunately for us, the professionals treating my child did know what to ask. For many children, these questions remain unspoken, and the reality of the child's feelings unrealized. When this pain is not identified and addressed, children seem to grasp for a way to express or demonstrate that they are hurting, sometimes by inflicting physical wounds on themselves. Self-hurting behaviors may also be sought in an effort to ease the internal hurt or inflict a perceived need for punishment.

> "When I was eight, I found a piece of broken glass in the back yard. I went out behind the garage and began cutting at my stomach." *Dale*

> "I crawled under my bed sobbing. I tried to take my safety scissors and cut my arms up. It did some damage, but not enough in my eyes. So I took my fingernails and scratched up my face." *Linda*

> "I have gone down the list of ways to hurt myself, and done them all. None of them were about dying, but about feeling like I was worth less than others." *Drew*

One man relayed to me an event that happened to him as a young child. He recalled having a long gravel driveway that was on a steep incline. He walked outside, took off his shirt and put on a helmet. He ran at full speed and dove onto the gravel driveway, sliding on his chest as the gravel tore at his skin. Unfortunately, even with such outward demonstrations, many parents still do not recognize the internal pain being experienced by the child. Dale, the 8-year-old above who cut at her stomach with glass, was never asked why she did so. She was spanked and simply told not to do it again, a common reaction for parents of her generation who knew little to nothing of this illness in children.

Internal Anger

Anger is an emotion we all experience. It is a reactive emotion for most of us. If you get fired from your job, you may feel angry. If a car runs a red light and narrowly escapes slamming into you, you may feel angry. The anger associated with bipolar disorder in children is different. It is an internal state of being that requires no outside prompting. It has a fuel all its own. The child must contend with this internal state without understanding why it exists. This internal anger is also reactive, but with higher intensity and less restraint. Throwing fuel on the fire will cause it to become totally explosive.

"When I get too angry, my brain goes black. I don't remember why I needed to rage. It's like it isn't me." *Tim, age 15*

"I had this internal rage that fueled and fueled and fueled. It only got worse by the minute. I could be in bed getting ready for sleep, and could have had a wonderful day. While I lay there waiting for sleep to come, I would just get very mad. The anger is worse than the depression. It can be very destructive." *Grace*

"When I was down, I was filled with hatred and was so miserable no one wanted to be around me." *Austin*

"As I got older, like 10-12, my depressions became more agitated." *Dale*

"My depression came out in irritability, anger and rages. One time, I put my arm through a window. Another, I threw a baseball bat through the wall when I was aiming for my brother's head. I broke nearly every piece of furniture in our apartment." *Bobbi*

"Whenever someone tried to provoke anger in me, or did something that I disliked, I would go into a blind frenzy like a cat in a fight. I would say horrible, devastating things that would deeply hurt someone else. It was like I removed myself from the situation. There were several episodes when I just simply went blank and did things I had no control over. When I finally had control of myself, my body shook all over and I sobbed so hard. Then, I usually ended up on the floor feeling so exhausted to the point I would have to drag myself to the bed. There was a different set of incidents that I could NOT remember what I did or said." *Vivian*

The intensity of it is exhausting, for all involved. The loss of control is frightening to witness, but also to experience. At times, the child's memory of the event is wiped away, as if it were simply too intense for the brain to process and keep. But the damage is not wiped away. Lost friendships, shame, tumultuous family life, hurt feelings, broken furniture and broken spirits are all the fruitage of this internal rage. Some of the most regrettable things happen in this state. What do children who experience this internal anger want you to know? Perhaps Eric, a 7-year-old boy, said it best.

"I wish that people knew how hard it is to be sad, and feel out of control." *Eric, age 7*

Through A Glass Wall

Few children with bipolar disorder feel that they can relate to the outside world. In many ways, they have difficulty even relating to themselves. They don't feel like they fit in, even with people who care for them. Especially during depression, the world seems to be passing them by, as if there is a barrier between them and everything else. Even in a room full of people they can feel totally alone.

> "I always felt like I didn't fit in at home or with peers, and I was on the inside of a glass wall looking out, but not really living or participating. The glass wall became a brick wall, and eventually was a comfort in knowing no one would get too close and know the real me." *Gina*

> "I didn't feel I had a place in this world. I had a very disconnected feeling from people, the world and myself." *Joan*

> "I would feel so empty inside me that I could not relate myself to anyone else. I felt as if I was an outsider, with no one acknowledging how sad I was. My childhood was more like a sole audience member, with all of the people in my life on a stage." *Vivian*

> "I felt that no one understood, or could ever understand, how I felt, because I didn't understand. No matter where I went or who I was with, I was alone." *Todd*

> "I would just stop wherever I was and watch the world exist, wondering how they all did it, and wonder why it seemed to come so easily for them." *Lee*

> "I often felt like I was an old, wise owl looking in on the world passing me by, like I never fit in. I often felt like I was having a sort of out-of-body experience, like I was not a part of my own life but watching someone on TV or reading about some character in a book." *Jordan*

> "I am a musician. When experiencing depression it seemed as if there was a film over my interaction with music. The passion and drive I had to create would be diminished significantly, though my music was still a safe haven for me. When the depression lifted, the passion and drive returned, sometimes with greater intensity, and always accompanied by great joy." *Margo*

> "Some of my earliest memories were of times we would all be sitting around the dining room table with friends or family, and I would start crying, because I felt so alone." *Alex*

This barrier, or disconnection, between the outside world and the child is one that sometimes is not only felt, but acted out. Drew and Todd both remember times when they felt compelled to do just that. These actions may not have been understood, but they were truly a picture into their inner feelings.

"Once, when I was 14 or 15 and had been depressed already for a year or so, all my friends were in my room hanging out and having fun. I spent the evening outside, looking in at them through the blinds. They just figured it was one of those weird things I did, but it was the only way I knew how to act out the numbness I was feeling." *Drew*

"I can remember one winter feeling very lonely and distant from everyone. I would dress all in black and walk or stand overlooking an open area, and just exist. Once, I walked for two hours up and down my street dressed all in black, including sunglasses, at 2 in the morning, in February, in the rain, trying to feel myself. I was lost and numb and couldn't feel myself." *Todd*

Making Decisions

Remember those catchy rhymes you said as a child to help you choose something when you couldn't decide? You know, the ones that start like, "Inky, binky, bonky ..." Of course they were silly, but sometimes they helped you decide between two or three things. All kids can have trouble making a decision, but as they grow, so does their decision making ability. For children with bipolar disorder, this difficulty with decision making goes to a whole new level. They become paralyzed with choices, and can't choose. The feelings here, as you will see, are both of being overwhelmed and fear of making the wrong choice.

"I've always felt unsettled in life, not being able to decide what I wanted to do. There were too many things to do; I would end up just sitting, or laying there, doing nothing." *Casey*

"I remember once being at McDonald's and practically having a panic attack over the fact that I could not decide what I wanted to eat. I knew the menu better than the Pledge of Allegiance. It became a major ordeal to me that I could not get beyond. I would become increasingly frustrated and finally just sit down, in tears, eating nothing at all, despite the fact that I was starving." *Jan*

"I couldn't make decisions at all. My concentration would go all to hell. I couldn't focus on school work or on the task at hand." *Drew*

"I had a hard time making decisions. I always felt like whatever choice I made was the wrong one, and I wanted to be sure I did the right thing. Little decisions seem huge." *Austin*

"I remember being unable to make simple decisions; my head felt fuzzy. I stressed out over whether or not I wanted Mountain Dew or Pepsi." *Miranda*

The adolescent years pose a special danger to those who have difficulty making decisions. There are peers who are quite willing to influence the indecisive one to his detriment. Before long, a teen can be heading down the wrong path and into disaster.

"When in a depressed state, I was indecisive about what I wanted to do. That would usually end up making me follow the crowd." *Joan*

So Tired!

With depression comes a loss of energy and a need for sleep. The feeling that accompanies this loss of energy is one of heaviness. Imagine that in every task you must perform there are weights added to your body. Your wrist feels like it has a ten-pound weight added to it, so that even picking up your pencil becomes a task that requires physical exertion. Walking is like trudging through mud up to your waist or, as Jill put it, "walking through pudding." You can see how even enjoyable activities become a huge task, requiring more energy than these children have to give.

> "Whenever depressed as a child, it seems to be a very big thing to be able to get anything out to play with, because I knew that I would have to then clean up when finished, and that seemed like an insurmountable task." *Linda*

> "I just didn't have the energy to go outside to play, or do anything else." *Carmen*

> "I felt so heavy. I felt drug down to the point of it being difficult to even sit up in a chair. I was afraid. I was incapable of doing anything but existing. I remember feeling like I was wading through quicksand, just pushing through something so very heavy. Just walking to another room was a challenge. Sitting up was hard. Speaking was too much." *Lee*

> "I hated being with others, and being in a crowd, and acting like I was happy all the time … it was too exhausting." *Jordan*

Along with the need for sleep due to physical exhaustion, there is a need to escape. For some, sleep becomes the escape, the place where the decisions, despair, anguish, blame and tears are temporarily kept at bay. Upon awakening, all the emotions rush in, making the desire to sleep look welcoming once again. The nothingness of sleep seems better than the alternative of awareness, and becomes a way to survive.

> "During my depressed days, I slept a lot. It seemed to be my escape from all the problems. I didn't want to deal with anyone or anything. I slept 12 or more hours, and then wanted to take naps during the day. My mom assumed I was lazy. I was having suicidal thoughts by the time I was 14. I was sure I wouldn't make it to 16. No one took me serious enough. No one told anyone; no one took it as a sign that something might be wrong." *Lee*

> "When I have been depressed, it feels like it is impossible to live life correctly, therefore, I wouldn't do anything at all. There was no point in doing life if I couldn't do it right. I would just shut down and stay in bed. I wanted nothing more than to sleep. I could sleep the day away." *Austin*

> "During depression, nothing could get me out of bed. I relished sleep, because that was all I had. It was, and has been, the only thing that kept me alive. The more I slept through my depression, the better the chance I had of getting through it. If I was awake, all I wanted to do was disappear. If it weren't for

sleep all those times, suicide would have seemed the only answer." *Rory*

A Heavy Burden

Life certainly comes with its difficulties. These are not easy times for children today. The once carefree childhood that many of us remember is nearly a thing of the past. Our children must deal with the reality of a harsh world, even at a young age. Families are broken, natural disasters displace children from homes, and the evening news brings the terror of the world right into the living room. This is a burden experienced by our youth today. For children growing up with bipolar disorder, the burden starts with life itself – life before the complications are added in. The normal, everyday tasks of life that others don't think twice about become a heavy burden.

"It seemed like I could never measure up to my own expectations. What should have been a very simple thing to the average child was a source of great frustration to me. I felt that if I couldn't accomplish such small, 'normal' goals, and behave similar to my peers, I had somehow not earned the right to be a part of the life they were living on Earth. I felt I was letting others down." *Jan*

"I felt like I was a very old woman who was ready to die. She had suffered enough living." *Abbey*

"Life was a heavy load, and I couldn't do it right. In fact, the load and burden of living was so difficult, and so big, that I didn't think I could accomplish it. I also didn't know how people could walk down the street looking so happy, because I didn't know that it wasn't this way for everyone." *Drew*

"When depressed, life is such a heavy load, such a burden. You feel you don't match up to your own expectations, or to those of others." *Olivia*

"I felt like life was a burden at times. It is like I never got to the point of being finished or accomplished. Every time I made some progress, then there was another step in front of me, but it usually had a negative feeling, and if something big and unexpected happened, I couldn't cope." *Todd*

"Ever since I can remember, just getting up every morning seemed to be such a chore that, some days, I would never leave my bed. Life was a job, not a privilege or a joy. Life was filled with work to do, people that counted on you, and you were too tired or sad to carry on." *Grace*

Now, add to these everyday normal things that have become burdensome an additional feeling, a feeling of great responsibility, a responsibility that stretches past reason and past the potential for success. This feeling is somewhat related to guilt, which we will talk about later, but I have included it here because of the strong way it causes these children to feel weighed down with burden.

You may be surprised by this feeling, as it goes somewhat contrary to what outsiders frequently conclude. If you are a parent of one of these challenging children, you have likely gotten notes home from school saying that little Johnny needs to "take responsibility" for his work. Or you may have had talks with your child about needing to "take responsibility" for chores, behavior or some such thing. These requests are targeted at changing a specific behavior. Adults often judge a child's feelings of responsibility by their ability to demonstrate those feelings through actions. At times, this illness limits a child's ability to make these changes, or express his feelings outwardly. This encourages some to believe that children with bipolar disorder just don't want to take responsibility and that they feel none.

The experience as seen and felt by the child is quite different. They feel such an overwhelming sense of responsibility about everything that they become paralyzed with the heavy weight of it. This deep sense of responsibility extends to things that are out of their control. It goes beyond reason, and it further weighs them down. These feelings of heavy responsibility cause them to give up before they ever start. Giving up, however, only adds to the misconception that they feel no responsibility to begin with.

> "I definitely experience a higher responsibility towards things and people in my life than the others I am around. I often become excited, and feel that the whole world rests on my shoulders. It is almost a 'bigger than life' feeling." *Miranda*

> "I have experienced all my life what I consider a deep sense of responsibility, not only for my own decisions, but for the health

and welfare of family, friends and those who I don't personally know." *Margo*

"I still, to this day, struggle with feeling responsible for other people. I would always want everyone to be happy, and I would go to great lengths to try and make that happen." *Alex*

"I always felt responsible for the fate of the world! It always felt like it was my responsibility to change the world and fix all the problems. I was afraid to live and make a mistake. It felt like a huge weight on my back every day, and it was too hard to carry it. I was afraid to live, and I was afraid to die, so I resented being brought into the world. Life was said to be this wonderful gift, but I saw it as a horrible burden. To me, living here was hell, and it had to be better to be dead. I used to actually ask people what they lived for! No one took me seriously, as the alternative seemed a non-option to them. I always felt living was a chore to be done each day, rather than a gift to be enjoyed." *Tasha*

Hopeless

Perhaps if a child had to experience such intense emotions, the feelings might be eased with the hope that soon he would feel better. Thus, we have the age old encouragement that surely the "sun will come out tomorrow." This saying is meant, of course, to inspire hope and a renewed spirit. Hope has enabled people suffering unspeakable things to endure. But children with bipolar disorder feel no hope and see no way out of their plight.

"I felt crazy and hopeless, and I wished someone understood me. I just seemed to suffer alone a lot. I would retreat on my own when depressed, and was incapable of getting help at all or expressing how I felt." *Jordan*

To them, there is no way out, no sun and no tomorrow. This feeling of hopelessness can quickly lead to what seems the only solution. Thoughts of dying can now become dreams of relief.

"There were numerous points of my childhood where I wanted to kill myself because of the deep depression." *Vivian*

"I felt so sad I wanted to kill myself, but I didn't want to." *Brian, age 9*

"Depression felt worse than dying. My father attempted suicide when I was 12 years old, because he too suffers from bipolar disorder. If I hadn't seen the damage his attempts caused me and my family, I too may have attempted suicide, but instead, I just suffered." *Miranda*

"I can remember learning the best way to slit my wrists so that they couldn't stop you if they caught you. I felt I was a coward because I couldn't go through with it. Later in life I did have an attempt." *Todd*

"I had a big obsession with ways to kill myself and with suicide in general, but never knew I could act on them. I imagined I was too much of a wimp." *Drew*

"I would think about dying, about the funeral, what death was like." *Austin*

One of the worst things about this illness is the way it makes children view themselves. There are illnesses that rob a child of health, vitality and length of days. Even in such cases, one may hear truly inspiring stories of courage, stories that demonstrate how, despite all, these children have not lost their spirit, their will to live and their desire to help others. Few illnesses are so cruel as to turn the child against his very being, but such is the case with bipolar disorder in children.

> "I always hated myself. I thought I was ugly." *Jill*

> "I always felt worthless, always. As a child, I felt that I was completely worth nothing, not worth caring for, feeding, even looking at." *Lee*

> "I had virtually no self-esteem and little or no confidence in myself." *Mark*

> "I have always felt worthless. I felt as though the world would be a better place without me, because I was becoming this burden on my friends and family. I felt as if nothing at all mattered." *Drew*

Waiting to Die

Some children not only hate themselves, hurt themselves and contemplate the relief that suicide seems to bring, but actually make a real attempt to end their pain. What feelings or thoughts precede such a desperate measure?

> "I felt very lonely. I felt I had no other choice. Suicidal thoughts feel like you are backed into a corner. The world, and pressures of it, can get to be too much to handle, and you feel like there isn't any other way out. You feel like you are being pushed into it, even though you logically know your family would miss you. You just feel pushed; just can't deal with things; they have become too much. Many things going on in my brain and I can't sort it all out, so it's all very jumbled, and then the pushy feelings can come. They are very, very, very overwhelming feelings, pushing you to suicidal thoughts." *Joan*

Those "overwhelming feelings" did push Joan to attempt suicide by swallowing a bottle of pills. Her parents never knew about the incident. They were not home and she called her boyfriend's mother, who instructed her to vomit. At age 16, Drew also attempted suicide by overdose and nearly died. Joan and Drew are not alone in their attempts. Some experts feel that as many as 30% of people diagnosed with bipolar disorder attempt suicide. Some will make several attempts. The statistics can be hard to establish because, as in the case of Joan, many suicide attempts go unrecognized and unreported.

Sadly, some of these attempts turn into fatalities. The risk of death in childhood bipolar disorder is very real, and outweighs the mortality rate of some childhood cancers. Statistics, however, can never tell the human suffering that leads to the attempt, nor the shame that comes after.

"One day, at age 14, I had to go shopping at the mall with my two older sisters and cousins. I hated public places and social situations when I was depressed. Somehow, these things made my depression worse. I tagged along behind my cousins and sisters, who were laughing and having a good time. I felt like I just wanted to be swallowed up by some hole in the ground and disappear. The lights, the music, the laughter, the sounds, it was all so over-stimulating and overwhelming to me. All these things were making me worse and worse.

My sisters and cousins were laughing at me, whispering and snickering. Who knows what they thought? I'm not even sure how I would have come across to myself when I was feeling 'normal.' I had a blank stare, a drawn, sullen face. My hair was greasy and unbrushed, my clothes oversized and mismatched. I didn't want to talk, I didn't want to go into stores, or look around. They all saw me as someone who did this for attention, trying to be the victim or trying to be weird. Didn't they know that if in an instant I could snap out of this hell I would? Didn't they know that the way I looked and acted were merely facades of how painful my depression was, indescribable, unimaginable? How could I ever express it and let everyone know just how much pain I was in?

I didn't talk and no one talked to me. When I got home, everyone scattered to go do other things. The house was empty, and I was alone. Impulsively, I took a bottle from the medicine cabinet, emptied all the blue little pills on the counter, poured myself a glass of apple juice, and stuffed all the pills into my mouth, drinking them down with apple juice until they were all gone; nothing left but an empty bottle of sleeping pills. I grabbed my blanket off my bed and went into the TV room. I curled up on the couch, closed my eyes, and waited to die. Sometime later, my sister came in the room. She kicked me and made some remark about me being a lazy ass. Completely drugged, I fell off the couch onto the floor. I couldn't move. I felt paralyzed. Everything was spinning and blurry. I started to vomit up blue.

My sister said, 'What the hell is wrong with you?' She called my mom at work. I just remember vaguely her talking to my mom and crying. My sister was saying, "What should I do? Are you coming home from work?" My mother never came home from work that day. She left my sister with me to take care of me by herself. Neither of them called an ambulance or poison control or a doctor, or even attempted to take me to the hospital. My mother had told my sister that as long as I kept vomiting, I would be OK. My sister got off the phone with my mom, came over and hugged me, and started to sob, 'Why did you try to kill yourself?'

I was so out of it, I couldn't move or speak. My ears were ringing, my vision was blurry, and I was dizzy and so exhausted. My sister kept trying to get me up off the floor. She tried to get me over the toilet to keep throwing up. She tried to make me get up and walk, saying that she wouldn't let me go back to sleep. My sister was inconsolable. She was crying and crying, and kept hugging me. 'Why would you do that?' she kept saying. Calling me by my nickname she'd say, 'I love you. You've got to stay awake. You can't go back to sleep.'

All I remember after that is trying to walk a straight line, my ears ringing loudly, dry heaving after all the blue pills were gone, and just wanting to fall asleep. I must have fallen asleep eventually because I slept for days. During the three to four days that I slept, I only vaguely remember my mother coming in to give me sips of water. I only saw her and my sister. The rest of the family was told that I was 'sick.' It was the secret my mother and sister and I kept from the family to this day." *Rory*

Suicide attempts are not limited to depressive episodes. We will talk later about manic and mixed states, but you should know that these too carry the risk of suicide. Perhaps the mixed state most of all, because the child not only feels depressed, but has the energy to carry out a suicide plan. Mark is one who stayed primarily in the manic states during childhood, yet he attempted suicide more frequently than any other person who shared their experiences with me. As he recovered from what he describes as a rare depressive episode and began to cross over into mania, his feelings intensified. For him, this was an especially dangerous time.

> "It is at these times I had intense feelings and irrational thoughts. By the age of 14, I had three serious suicide attempts, and was hospitalized for over a year. I have made approximately eighteen serious suicide attempts, beginning at age 13." *Mark*

It's My Fault Again

Rory's attempt to take her life was followed by "tremendous guilt." Children with bipolar disorder can have feelings of guilt over actions directly related to their illness, no matter the mood state. One woman noted that a child's feelings of guilt may not be obvious to an onlooker. Speaking from experience, she said that after a mood episode has passed, there is a great deal of embarrassment and guilt that seems to push them "*farther into the dark, dark hole that we try so hard to escape.*"

> "During times that I did things that were out of control, or when I was so depressed that I was unable to function, I felt extremely guilty. It only brought what little self esteem I had down even further." *Lee*
>
> "When I would have an episode, I would get upset and start yelling, screaming, swearing and saying mean things which I didn't mean. Then, I felt so terribly guilty and ashamed about what I did and said that I truly wanted to die. Afterwards it is so humiliating, because you can remember people's looks and whispers, and you know they think you are a bad person." *Bobbi*
>
> "My guilt came when my father had to come and bail me out from manic episodes." *Mark*
>
> "I felt guilty for being depressed, because it would add to the family burden of my mother's depression. So I hid it." *Jill*

In addition to feelings of guilt and embarrassment over episodes, guilt is an expression of depression itself. As you'll see next, it doesn't take a major event for children with bipolar disorder to experience a heavy guilt. While they may feel guilt for something they've said or done, oftentimes, the guilt may be over something very abstract, like the problems of the world. Lee felt guilty for eating at times. Olivia felt similarly, and said that even breathing made her feel guilty!

"Often, I would lay awake at night going over how many mistakes I made in the day, and replaying things I said that I should not have said." *Drew*

"I have always thought I was supposed to 'do' something, but never knew what, and then felt as though I couldn't do anything because someone else could do it better anyway. I thought everything was my fault. I would always blame myself for things I really had no control over but thought I, somehow, had done something to bring this about." *Joan*

"I felt like I'd have a heart attack with all the guilt I felt. If I did something minor that I felt might disappoint someone, or even myself, I'd feel extreme stress and guilt over it. I felt totally worthless and almost paranoid … like everyone knew how much I was a screw-up." *Jordan*

"I would get very depressed if others were sad and I would oftentimes feel guilty, as if I had done something to cause the problem. It didn't matter if I did anything wrong, I still felt to blame for everything that was wrong." *Alex*

"The guilt was unbearable. I seemed unable to forgive myself for trivial things that children go through growing up. I felt that I should have sent apology notes to everyone that knew me. I felt guilty and worthless about the fact of what I was putting my family through." *Miranda*

These guilt feelings experienced by children with bipolar disorder carried over strongly into their adult lives. Many of their comments, even in adulthood, resonated with guilt and shame. One woman recalled her childhood reaction when a new baby was brought into the household. While her actions and feelings might have been quite comparable to many 7-year-old children who are adjusting to a new sibling, Grace says, "Even to this day the guilt strikes when I think back about it."

Final Thoughts

In the beginning of this section, Marty described the depressive phase of bipolar disorder as "darkness within." The feelings discussed in this section all come together to form this darkness. Most of us have opened our eyes in a dark room and, as our eyes slowly adjust, we start to make out shadows and shapes. While this could be described as "dark," it is not the "darkness" you have learned about here. This darkness is a complete and overwhelming darkness, with no outside light source to illuminate the way. It's the type of darkness that exists in caves and caverns. No matter how wide you open your eyes or how long you stare, there is nothing but darkness. That is the darkness referred to by Marty. It is an internal darkness so complete that the child cannot find his or her way out; a darkness that strikes fear and panic into the hearts and minds of these young ones.

Any one of the intense feelings in this depressive phase could be debilitating. Put together, they are formidable. You may be emotionally tired from just reading the experiences here. Imagine living them. Not living them now, as an adult, but suffering through them as a child. Imagine not knowing or understanding that these feelings are not a normal part of every person's existence. Imagine not being able to express yourself in order to get help. Imagine people negating your experience because you are a child. It's not a pretty picture. It's one that makes me wish desperately that I could turn back the hands of time in order to stop the suffering of these children. I want to reach onto these pages and intervene, to tell the children that there is hope. That is not possible. But I can tell you, the reader, in the hopes that you will reach out to the children in your life who may be suffering. Perhaps you will open your heart to understand, and extend your hand to help.

Depression is only one phase of bipolar disorder. We have just begun to address everything encompassed by this illness. We have only covered the first aspect of this emotional roller coaster ride. Next, we will consider the opposite "pole" in bipolar disorder: mania. While you will find it considerably different from the depressive phase, it is no less devastating or heartbreaking.

Keep in mind as we leave depression to discuss mania that children don't get to leave it so easily. They have no warning when depression will lift and mania will begin. They can't flip a page in a book to change their mood state.

SECTION 2

Mania

"Itchy twitchy in my skin
Growing flowing deep within

Twirly swirly thoughts alight
Inhibitions take to flight

Each sound, each smell, each drop of light
In these my soul does take delight

I play with them, they intermingle
In each pore they bring a tingle

Intoxication of the senses
I drink it in as life itself and fear its end as death

I must give in, I must obey
Before it then is taken away

Imploding, exploding, searing pain
For all else there is disdain

Crashing, smashing through my brain
Pain
Pain
Pain"

Dawn Schwarz

Riding the Wave

Interrupted by the sound of unrestrained laughter, my conversation came to an abrupt halt. The laughter silenced the rest of the crowded room as it punctuated the air. Several people turned to investigate the source of this disturbance. Across the room, a group of young people were smiling and chuckling. There, in the middle of the group, sat my son, laughing uncontrollably. As he continued on for some time, the atmosphere became uncomfortable. Tears were spilling over and running down his face, while the laughter gave no indication of letting up. His peers went from chuckling to stale smiles, as they watched with interest to see how long my son could maintain this laughter.

It was nice to hear him laugh, yet disturbing. It marked not a beginning of wellness, but another part of his illness – mania. Mania is a deceiver. It arrives with promises of relief from the darkness of depression. It masquerades as goodness and light, only to betray the child. It is a wave rising higher and higher, threatening to overtake everything. It tosses them to dangerous heights, unrestrained by reality, only to crash back down into the depths of despair.

> "Experiencing the manic side as a child felt like pure elation, like life couldn't be better. Cycling up is like body surfing the most incredible wave you can imagine on a beautiful sunny day. Cycling down hard is like being caught in an undertow during a storm. Everything else is just somewhere in between." *Olivia*

> "The wave goes higher and higher but, like all waves, it has to eventually break. Then it crashes over and goes all the way down, washing up on shore. Hopefully the surf stays low and no more waves start." *Jill*

Move It, Move It

When children with bipolar disorder experience mania, they have an increased level of energy. Energy is the force that drives us. When this energy or force is elevated, the child's physical activity is also elevated. How does all this increased energy feel to children who are in a manic state? It's a great feeling – initially. It feels as if the weights of depression have dropped to the floor, and nothing can keep them bound to the Earth. Their spirits soar like an eagle. However, the energy that was a friend soon becomes a Master. The child must move, not because he wants to, but because this energy demands a release.

> "I would toss and turn and have the feeling that my skeleton was going to simply burst through my skin unless I got up and did something." *Grace*

> "I had so much energy I just wanted to jump and run around. It was like I couldn't control my body. I would lie there just trying not to jerk my limbs or scream. My mother would say I was like a monkey swinging all over the house." *Austin*

> "I wanted to just run … run away from everything; my life, my family, everything. Sometimes I wanted to start physically running and never stop. No destination in mind, just running from something." *Lee*

If we imagine these children running, jumping, climbing and swinging on a playground, this seems just fine. But let's take the same children and imagine them at Aunt Betty's luncheon or in Miss Manners' classroom. No matter how hard they try to exercise restraint, manic energy will not be contained. The result at every turn is disapproval: disapproval from parents, teachers, relatives, friends and, perhaps most heartbreaking of all, disapproval from themselves.

Swirling Thoughts

Thinking is an amazing part of the human experience. It allows us to learn, reflect, imagine and create. Thoughts are part of our private identity. They can allow us to be in the moment or experience a daydream that can take us halfway around the world. Our thoughts can soothe us, or accuse us. The energy in mania does not stop with a physical need to move, but stretches into a child's private identity. Thoughts now become accelerated, as if running through their head. This creates a whirlwind of activity, as ideas and images race through the brain. Just as with the physical aspect, this feels exciting and enjoyable to the child, initially.

> "I loved it and always wanted it to last forever. It is usually on the exhilarating side because I feel smarter, sharper and able to recall and relay memories and feelings easier." *Rory*

> "I have always had racing thoughts, and really enjoyed it. It is exciting to have all these ideas and ambitions in your mind. I always made sure I wrote everything down. I was so afraid I would forget something important. I would go off on tangents, researching and investigating." *Austin*

> "I always thought flight of ideas was fun. I could think rings around other people, although I was often making no sense to them." *Mark*

Soon, however, the deceit sets in. The thoughts come faster and faster, with no way to sort through or express them. What seems at first to be exhilarating, pleasant and fun, now becomes a free-for-all in the brain. The thoughts will not shut off. This is a very internal experience, and difficult to describe to someone not experiencing it firsthand. It's as if the child is standing in the middle of an invisible circle of people. Each person is speaking as quickly and loudly as possible about a variety of subjects. One voice is singing rhymes, another is contemplating the fate of the universe, a third is babbling nonsensically, another is narrating the morning's events, yet another is dialoguing about possible inventions, and so on. If you were in the middle of this circle, you would likely be moved to the point of screaming for everyone to stop. At the very least, you would walk away. Walking away solves nothing for the child. These aren't outside people or voices. They are the child's own racing thoughts. To the child, this experience becomes overwhelming and frustrating. When Steven, an 11-year-old boy, was asked what it feels like to have so many thoughts at once, he said that it made him feel confused, overwhelmed, anxious and afraid.

> "It would feel like a train running thru your head moving at top speed, and your body can't keep up." *James*

> "It feels like I don't know what to do all of the time, because I don't know what thought to pick in my head. They are all scrambled." *Alisha, age 7*

"I have many thoughts in my head. It is very scary. I feel like I am becoming a gorilla. I feel out of control, because I can't think clearly. I become angry. Sometimes I feel silly. I become very stubborn. Many feelings happen inside me, and I do not like it." *Andrew, age 10*

"I often tell people that my disease is the thinking disease, because I am always thinking and can't shut my mind up. When I am manic or hypomanic, my ideas are very flighty and just jump around and go in circles. I felt so dizzy and cluttered in my brain. I couldn't get anyone to understand how fast I was thinking, and how I just thought about everything. When I would draw or write to illustrate my thinking, other people said it overwhelmed them, because it was too busy or fast or colorful. They couldn't process it, but to me it was calming because I was expressing how crazy I felt in my brain. I often felt my thinking was going in circles. I would go from one idea to the next to the next, and eventually end up back at the beginning to rethink it. During these times I often said that my theme song was the oldie: 'I'm so dizzy my head is spinning, like a whirlpool it's never ending." *Drew*

"When my thoughts start racing I can become agitated and not know why. I have many thoughts going around in my head, but can't sort through them, making me very agitated." *Joan*

"I remember having many racing thoughts, to the point that my thoughts and ideas would bounce from one thought to another." *Lee*

"Racing thoughts are pesky and tiring. Sometimes they have been words repeating, or rhyming words in my thoughts, not out loud. They would just be there. For a long time I thought that this was just how everybody thought. It wasn't until I was medicated that I realized most people don't have that static in their brain." *Olivia*

> "My head would spin sort of inside." *Jordan*

Now let's take this a step further and invite the child into a situation that requires him to listen or concentrate. The thoughts don't stop with the increased expectations. Concentration becomes a superhuman effort. As you will see in the following quotes, it is one that often meets with failure.

> "My thoughts could race so much that I wouldn't be able to think straight or concentrate on anything, because there would be many thoughts going around in my head at once. It's like everyone who needed me to answer a question or needed me to do something for them and everything that I needed to do was all swirling around in my mind in a big ball. Every once in a while I could catch a thought, but I couldn't do anything about that thought because of all the swirling." *Joan*

> "The racing thoughts have affected my relationships and communications with others. I'm so consumed with thoughts in my head that when I am talking to someone I don't really remember everything. I am trying to register what they are saying, and I'm also thinking about the things in my head. I try hard to focus on them and the conversation, but I am thinking about so many different things that I'm only in the moment with that person. Once the conversation is over, I realize I don't remember much of what was said. The info isn't really registering on a deep level." *Austin*

> "It was hard to concentrate, and the thoughts would swirl in my head, especially if I was anxious. In conversations, I wouldn't be sure what was said." *Gina*

Let's Talk

Parents and relatives are thrilled when a child says "dada" or "mama" for the first time. Talking is an integral part of life. Through it a child communicates his needs and enjoys interaction with other people. In many ways our speech defines us to the outside world. It is how we let others know who we are. Through it we develop relationships, convey our thoughts and leave an impression on others. Because of this, our speech becomes part of our identity. When a child with bipolar disorder is manic, he feels a strong pressure to talk. Like all things manic, it can feel exhilarating at first.

> "I become very talkative during my manic state; honestly it felt great, considering that during my depressed state I felt nothing was worth talking about. I remember my grandmother pointed it out to me, and I became upset. I remember thinking, I'm so happy, why can't she be happy for me." *Miranda*

> "When I would be talking in junior high school it did feel exhilarating, almost like a high." *Jordan*

What seems to be happy, good and wonderful to the child now becomes a huge problem. Just as the thoughts race and refuse to slow down, talking gets out of control as well.

The child feels compelled to speak, just as he felt compelled to move. The child's speech can hardly keep up with his thoughts as they race through the mind. Conversation then can be difficult for the young person, because there is a frustration in trying to convey thoughts. The child bounces from one topic to another and may confuse those around him.

> "I was always known as the motor mouth by my group of friends. In fact, one of my friends in the sixth grade got a shirt for me that said, "Help! I am talking and I can't shut up." You never completely finish a story you were talking about before you so quickly change the subject. When talking to friends, if there was ever a quiet pause of any type, you felt that you had to interject and keep the conversation going. Sometimes the thoughts would run so fast through my head I would think I told the person something but I did not, I had only thought about it. The only way I knew to try and fix this was to try and sit quietly. This never worked. The urge, need and pressure were so intense." *Grace*
>
> "I talked constantly." *Todd*
>
> "Talking to people was very difficult at times, due to the fact that I would skip from one subject to another, leaving them lost and dumbfounded, and me not having a clue that I had even done it." *Lee*
>
> "I looked like the doll Chatty Cathy." *Gina*
>
> "When manic, I feel like my speech keeps up with my thoughts, and I can't slow it down. Because I think so quickly, and in such a roundabout manner, I have to keep talking to keep my ideas flowing." *Drew*

> "I feel like I have to answer/ask/voice all the thoughts or questions going through my head at the time. That's why I talk so much all the time and ask so many questions all at once." *Brian, age 9*

If you think excessive talking is not a really big deal to experience, think again! Unlike racing thoughts, which is a very private experience, talking involves other people. It's not something you can hide, and it leaves its mark everywhere. Both peer interaction and interaction with teachers and parents are affected. This symptom becomes a truly embarrassing aspect of the illness for some children. It elicits very strong feelings and memories, even into adulthood.

> "My speech could never keep up with my thoughts. My own mind couldn't seem to keep up. On the one hand, it was quite exhilarating to have such a busy mind, but on the other hand, it was very frustrating not to be able to get my point across to others. It was so frustrating at times that it led to my becoming an introvert in social scenes rather than embarrass myself trying to share the many ideas with others." *Erin*

> "In first grade I often got my mouth taped shut (by the teacher) because I talked too much." *Jill*

> "You know you talk too much. Sometimes you say too much. You feel that everyone looks at you and wants to say SHUT UP. If you were not talking, you felt that others would not think of you as important. It was a very sad feeling at times, and when in a very high mania it was very nerve-racking for others." *Grace*

"I would talk about anything. I would start talking and then midway through start feeling so stupid because I knew I really had nothing important to say and no one was really interested in hearing it. But I couldn't find a way to stop, so I would continue on, feeling more and more pressure to keep on going and to find a way to make it interesting, and to find a way to make them listen." *Lee*

Sleep. Who Needs It?

Do you ever remember sneaking out of bed as a child because you didn't want to go to sleep and miss something? I used to hide behind my father's reclining chair and watch television until I was caught and promptly sent to bed. But once tucked in bed, it was just a matter of time before I could no longer fight to hold my eyelids open. Few children really want to go to bed, and sleep eludes all of us from time to time. However, unlike my experience, where the right conditions brought on sleep, children who are experiencing the increased physical and mental energy of mania just can't seem to shut down. They may fight to hold their eyelids shut, but their minds and bodies are wired. Sleep, then, becomes a real issue. When Todd was a teenager, he wrote the following poem, which captures his frustrations regarding sleep.

"As I linger in my cold bed,
I know not what it is I dread.
I keep remembering everything said.
Thoughts, emotions run deep.
Some applies to me, some I set free.
If thoughts would just let me be,
I could get some sleep."

Todd Schwarz

Others could relate to Todd's experience and commented on their feelings, in addition to frustration, that came with the lack of sleep.

"I had so much energy. When I went to bed sometimes I felt like I wanted to crawl out of my skin." *Austin*

"There were many nights I could not sleep." *Mark*

"When I got older and into my teens, nights of not sleeping increased." *Alex*

"I had racing thoughts as a child and teen. They always seemed to come flooding in during the middle of the night. What an adrenaline rush it would be!" *Jan*

"It was hard to sleep because so many ideas were floating in my head. I barely slept, and I was living on the edge of sanity." *Miranda*

"During my manic days I would be up all night, little or no sleep needed, and much energy, but at times feeling a strange exhaustion, but wired." *Lee*

While the feelings range from frustration, crawling out of one's skin, an adrenaline rush, and wired exhaustion, they all result in the same thing; little sleep. And what do these children do during this time at night? Do they lie idly in their beds awaiting the dawn? Sometimes this might be the case, but frequently they have secret activities which may be unknown to their parents.

> "I would be up all night cleaning the leaves on silk plants, or playing games. My parents never knew I was up. I would stay in my room, read and play games." *Lee*

> "As early as I can remember, I never really slept well. Sometimes I wrote stories and sometimes I made 'books' about real subjects. I also wrote poetry and song lyrics. If something came to me when I was lying in bed trying to sleep, I HAD to get up and write it down. This happened a lot! I think I always had trouble falling asleep, and I would lay there and think. My most expressive and creative ideas came to me then. Often, I'd get up in the middle of the night and dance. I'd read a story called 'The Seven Dancing Princesses,' and I'd pretend to be one of them. They snuck out at night and danced until their shoes were worn out. I didn't stay up that long, but I did twirl around a bit before settling down to try to sleep again! During the school year I was up doing homework, which I had trouble doing during the daytime. Sometimes I would come out of my room when everyone was asleep and clean the house!" *Tasha*

> "I would awake and sit at the desk in our room coloring, creating paper pictures, etc." *Marty*

> "I would spend a lot of time writing and listening to music. I would be extremely happy and funny at these times." *Alex*

"During mania, I rarely slept. My parents didn't know that I was up all night long. I would be downstairs in my bedroom reading or drawing all night, listening to music. Sometimes I snuck out and went to the park to carve castles and animals in the sand, thinking how great it would all look in the morning when kids came to the park to play. 'Who was this artist that came in the night and made creatures out of the sand?' they would all say." *Rory*

Projects

Whether it is night or day, this manic energy must have an outlet. During the day, it may be viewed as somewhat more acceptable. Friends may even find this energy contagious. The child may lock onto several ideas that then must be carried out. This can result in very creative expression. It can also result in obsessive or stuck thinking, which takes possession of the child's focus and refuses to let go. Like a pit bull that bites down and locks its jaw, the young person locks onto a project, idea or item to buy.

"I would begin projects such as putting together outfits for the next four weeks, rearranging my room, writing poetry, and beginning my novel, and so forth." *Grace*

"These were my most creative times, when I was manic and unable to sleep. I painted the best, wrote the best stories and poems, and felt the best, because it seemed the less I slept the sharper and more aware I became." *Rory*

"When I was a teen, I remember my parents saying, 'You get an idea in your head and you don't let it go.' That was so true. I would carry on until I got what I wanted, not because I was spoiled, but once I got an idea in my head, I couldn't get rid of it. Even if I no longer wanted the thing, I would still carry on. When I am in task mode, I don't like to be touched. It freaks me out. I feel like a prickly cactus." *Austin*

When mania abates, the child no longer has the energy necessary to complete all that he set out to do. Unfinished projects now leave the child with a strong sense of failure, even though the original expectations were self-imposed and may not have been attainable or realistic to begin with.

"I would either work so hard to finish the projects that I would literally make myself ill, or I would have multiple projects going on that were left unfinished. I would go crazy knowing they were not complete, but not having the energy to move forward." *Grace*

"When you start all those projects, it then takes a while to finish them, because then the thoughts race and you can't organize what you need to do to accomplish the project. This can be sooo frustrating, and then you feel overwhelmed." *Joan*

"When I first experienced mania, I got other people around me excited about things that were going on, however, I never really followed through with anything at a steady pace." *Miranda*

Altered Reality

In addition to increasing mental and physical energy, mania alters the thinking patterns and perceptions of young people. Reality is skewed and false beliefs take over. This feels normal to the child, as if it truly is reasonable and real. All of us respond to our environment based on our reality. If you are a common person experiencing life in a common way, you will act differently from the President of the United States. But what if you are a common person whose altered perception tells you that you are the President? Your actions now become out of context, as you act in a way that seems appropriate to your reality which is, in fact, very far from actual reality. To the casual observer it may seem a farce. To the child, it is real.

> "I believed I had the ability to broadcast my thoughts and cause other people to act as I wanted them to act. All my life I've felt someone was watching me. I felt like there were cameras in the rooms or the TV was two-way, or somehow someone was observing all I did. I did not feel at peace when I was alone." *Tasha*

> "Sometimes I would believe I had super powers, or that I was able to do things that other people couldn't, like see actual atoms in the air, or know how many napkins were in a pile on the table." *Olivia*

"I really thought I was a princess, and my parents had me hidden away until I was of the age of 18! This stayed with me from about 4 years until pre-teen. I felt that all of the people around me were really my bodyguards. I was above everyone else, and I was feeling awfully good. It was a great high. I loved that feeling of being the best. In these moods you may have a hateful, mean streak, but you are in a pretty good mood. It was one of the better moods. At least you loved yourself." *Grace*

"I remember swinging on the swing set, and swinging as hard as I could. I knew I could fly if I could go high and fast enough. I felt I could swoop down over our house, and watch my crazy world going on below me, and not have to be there. I always felt during those moments 'out of me' and watching over it all, but happy and powerful and in control. Swinging high, climbing as high as I could climb, and running as fast as I could." *Lee*

"There was a time I believed that I could control or insert my ideas into people's minds, and that I could read their minds." *Dawn*

This altered reality can prove dangerous at times. When a young person doesn't have the ability to perceive reality accurately, they no longer have recognition of certain dangers. For instance, if a child's altered reality tells him that he has the ability to fly, he may jump from a high place, such as a window or a tree. This may have nothing to do with a desire to be hurt, though the possibility of injury is quite real.

"I also believed that I could control my body's response to temperature to the point that I put my hand into boiling water once, believing I would not be hurt." *Tasha*

I'm Superior

Having good self-esteem is vital for all of us. How we view ourselves is important to our success. We have already seen that in the depressive phase, young people with bipolar disorder have little self-esteem and, in fact, can even hate themselves. In the manic phase, children go to the opposite extreme, with inflated self-esteem.

> "I can remember, in the second grade, drawing pictures of alligators and signing them and giving them to people I knew so that they would have something of mine, because I was going to be famous one day, and then they would have something valuable." *Todd*

> "I experienced inflated self esteem; however, I'm sure I looked like an idiot to the people who cared about me, especially my family. I remember feeling like my life was so great, when it really wasn't at all. When I became manic my little sister started to pick up on the symptoms, and believed something wasn't right. She stopped by a friend of mine's house to check on me, and my sister said I was just way too happy. I was simply frying an egg and acting like I was saving the world." *Miranda*

Mixing this with the child's altered reality is a recipe for grandiosity. This goes well beyond self-esteem. It is a feeling of superiority which, in turn, means that normal bounds and rules do not apply. How does this grandiosity affect a young person's interaction with others? Grandiosity in mania may look very haughty and disrespectful. The child is not afraid to question the validity of anyone else in authority over them, including parents and teachers. The young person truly feels that he is, indeed, superior to everyone around him, whether these are peers or adults. Grandiosity makes a young person feel totally justified in questioning everyone and everything. Interactions with other people become strained at best.

> "While more often than not I felt like crap about myself and didn't think I should be alive, my mania began with little thoughts and actions of grandiosity. I would come up with these totally wacky ideas and just go off on them and expect everyone to listen. I decided that my thinking and ideas were just at a higher level than others and that they just couldn't understand. I felt I was chosen or special to have all these thoughts and see different parts of things that others couldn't." *Drew*

> "I had the feeling that others just weren't as mentally advanced as me and couldn't get what I was talking about, or that I must have been smarter, because, to me, all my ideas meant I was imaginative and intelligent." *Erin*

> "I could do things that others couldn't, therefore making me feel better than these simpletons." *Dawn*

Hallucinations

The experience of an altered reality can go a step further in mania and include seeing, hearing, smelling, tasting or feeling things that are not real. At times the child does seem to recognize that these events are not reality. Other times, there is a firm belief that these experiences are real. One young man could differentiate between his auditory hallucinations and "real" sounds, because the hallucinations were "louder" to him. How did that make him feel? Even with the knowledge that it was not real, he was very fearful. He no longer would go outside or into the bathroom alone. Others describe the feeling as "creepy" or "uncomfortable."

> "Whenever I was in mania and washing my face, I would 'see' a man in the reflection on the faucet. It was more of a fracture of a man. I remember the creepy sensation it gave to me. It sort of became a dare for me. I tried to catch that man in the mirror when I raised my head really fast. Of course, I would never catch him in the mirror. Yet I kept on doing this. I also would expect to see him around the corner of walls. When the room was dark, I would become hysterical and run to the source of light in fear that the guy would catch me. It took counseling before I could let go of that hallucination." *Vivian*

> "My hallucinations seemed to involve all of the senses … I recall not only seeing but also hearing, smelling and feeling an

indescribable 'aura.' Feeling an 'aura' is the worst. This 'aura' I describe could be compared to what some call an out-of-body experience. Sometimes, I would look down at my hands, or something, and it felt like they belonged to somebody else. It's creepy and makes me jumpy for the rest of the day." *Jan*

"My auditory hallucinations can best be described as hearing a radio very close to my ear, but no one else hears the radio. My voice generally gave me positive, creative ideas; however, the voice would give command hallucinations about hurting myself and, occasionally, others. Although I made many suicide attempts, obviously I never succeeded, and I never hurt anyone else." *Mark*

"The hallucinations and altered thinking is what alerted me that something was terribly wrong. I didn't feel comfortable anywhere I was, and I lost a lot of sleep that I feel may have caused the hallucinations." *Miranda*

There are some major misconceptions when it comes to the area of hallucinations and altered reality. The populace in general is inclined to believe that young people experiencing this would be so far out of their minds that it would be quite apparent to the outsider. The reality is that an outsider may not be aware of the experience at all.

"Once, when I was in fourth grade, I was standing in line to go to class. When I looked at the girl in front of me, I saw a different face on her head than normal. I never told the teacher what I saw. Nobody knew until I told my mom later. I was afraid to tell anyone else." *Rick, age 13*

Some people actually refuse to believe that a child is telling the truth about such experiences, and even punish a child for sharing them. This is truly a sad misconception that must be changed. Hallucinations, although not always present, can be a very real symptom of bipolar disorder in children. The experience can be exacerbated by stress.

> "I saw bats, a knife with blood, and a man with a gun. It was very scary. They would go away and come back. When I was upset or under a lot of pressure, they would come back. Once, I had a math test that made me really nervous. Then, I started seeing the bats again. My teacher thought I was trying to get out of taking a test, but I wasn't making it up." *Savannah, age 14*

> "When I was about six or seven, I was staying at my grandparents' home in Georgia. I had to sleep upstairs in an attic style bedroom alone. I saw a 'roach motel' box thing, and was upset when my grandma told me what it was. I began to obsess about not sleeping in this room. I was crying and they told me I had to go up there and see that it was safe and there were no bugs. I begged to not go up, but they insisted. I finally entered the room and, to this day, I remember it vividly. I saw a huge bug on the wall. It was bright green, one of those walking stick type bugs that look like a blade of grass, but this one was about ten feet long from head to bottom and about four feet wide! Its antennas were wiggling, and its head moved some. It was on the wall near the bed I was to sleep in, filling up the whole wall from corner to corner. When I saw the antennas move, I screamed like I'd been murdered and almost passed out, but was able to run back down the stairs. I was almost hyperventilating. My family members obviously didn't believe this 'story' and thought I was making it all up, and even teased me some. However, I didn't have to sleep up there. I will never forget this bug." *Jordan*

Reckless

As we grow into adulthood, many of us realize just how naïve we were as children. We may look back and wonder how we survived some of the choices we made as a teen. But normal teenage years still have at least a measure of restraint based on the child's reality, beliefs and experience. What, then, if our reality lies to us? A child or teen experiencing altered reality may have a strong belief he is invincible, that danger doesn't apply to him. He does not respond to the urging of peers who sense the danger. Without the normal restraints in place, this becomes a particularly dangerous time.

> "It is almost a larger than life experience, because you feel that you can conquer anything." *Miranda*

> "I remember one night in particular when I was 16. I sat on the roll bar of a friend's Jeep while he four-wheeled through some huge hills on the property, driving 45-50 miles per hour. It was so scary to my friends that they screamed at me the entire time to get down. I was invincible. I was as good as a queen. I was the best, and nothing could hurt me. I just wonder how many teenage deaths that are caused by recklessness are a result of a bipolar teen." *Grace*

> "I often put myself in very dangerous situations. I thought I was invincible. The behavior manifested in doing dangerous, but

often exciting, things. When I was about 15, I received a new bike for my birthday. One day, I decided to ride my bike to Florida. My first obstacle was getting through a tunnel. I got turned away several times. I figured that if I held on to the back of a truck, the police wouldn't see me. Was I wrong! Waiting on the other side of the tunnel was the police, en masse. My father was not too happy about bailing me out of that one. I finally did make it to Florida. I 'borrowed' my father's American Express card. I realized I had to get a job. I got a job overseeing the (fruit) pickers. I was only 16, and some of the workers were much older than me. This seemed like an injustice to me, so I organized the pickers to strike. We were all arrested and put in a hell-hole of a jail. They agreed to release me to my father, but the others would have to stay. I refused to leave, and remained in jail for four months. Both my parents were waiting for me when I was released. They said they were very proud of me. However, they knew it was a manifestation of my manic depression." *Mark*

Sexual Impulse

The intensity of feelings in mania does not stop short when it comes to sexual matters, even in very young children. We have already discussed both physical and mental energy, and how they drive everything in mania. Sexual feelings are also driven beyond normal realms, with the release never being enough. Due to the overtly sexual behavior of very young children in mania, outsiders sometimes wrongly conclude that the child has been molested. This relates back to our need for explanation through cause and effect. Just as the pain in depression is a result of the illness itself, heightened sexual impulses come as a result of mania. Age is no longer the determining factor for sexual desire to be awakened. But when normal teenage awakening meets increased sexual desire in mania, there is an explosion of intensity! Out of respect for those who shared these feelings in such a private matter, names have been left off entirely.

> "I remember the high sexual drive. It was an overpowering feeling, and it took over the primary thought and feeling in me. As a child I would masturbate constantly when I would get into those manic phases. I just couldn't help it. It always felt like I had to do something about that feeling, like I could have an orgasm very quickly, and over and over. Even in my childhood days, I could have been touched by a boy or a girl, it didn't really matter, only that I 'needed' to be touched and have that release. I am not bisexual, but it was all about being touched, not who was doing the touching. But then they had to do it to me over and over a few times, because that feeling would just keep coming back. I ended up in really bad situations concerning sex, because during those phases, I would seem to be acting more 'sexy,' so guys or boys back then would think that I wanted sex from them. I always had a not-so-good reputation, but I really wasn't like that at all."

> "I would sneak out my window and into the city. This was from about age 14 forward. I would find women of the evening."

> "I became boy crazy at an early age and sexually promiscuous, ending up pregnant at 15."

"I somehow lost control of my sex life. It still, today, is hard for me to understand how a sweet young girl, all of a sudden, would sleep with anyone, and not once worry about the consequences."

"As a teenager, I was very promiscuous. I enjoyed the excitement of being with someone new. It was like a high. I would sleep with anyone: men I had just met, married men, men much older than me, etc. I didn't care. It made me feel good."

"I went through very promiscuous times as a young teen and through college. It was not who I felt I really was, and it was humiliating to me. I felt extreme guilt and shame over this."

Along with the increased sexual drive in mania, some young people with bipolar disorder describe sex as an addiction that gives them a temporary high, lifting the pain momentarily. When the high is gone and the reality of the emotions is still present, relief is sought once again.

"I lost my virginity at age 14 to a 35-year-old married man that I met and only knew for an hour, and never saw again. It is very painful to bring any of this up, because I would like to forget it all. The pain is only briefly gone during the sex itself, but returns full strength once over. While the men and boys may want you, they don't respect you, and once they've gotten what they want, you are nothing to them, and become nothing to yourself. You keep repeating the sexual behavior hoping that next time will be different and all your pain will go away, not just during the sex but after, and finally you will feel happy or complete. I used my body and sexuality as a tool to get what I needed: enough attention from boys or older men to feel wanted for a little while. This became an addiction for me to heal the pain. Like drugs, the high is always there to relieve you and make you forget, but the lows are waiting. When it's over you feel worse than before, and this drives you to want more. 'Maybe just one last time and then I will be OK,' until you hit rock bottom and say, 'No more!' But that's hard when you have bipolar, because your moods play tricks on you. When you are manic you just don't care, and you start it all over again. Then you become depressed, and depend on the sex to get you through it. This was going on throughout my teenage years, and nobody ever knew about it."

Need for Control

Control is an important part of life. But what if you no longer have control? Imagine driving a car. When you try to apply the brakes, you go faster. When you turn on the windshield wipers, the horn blares. When you pull out and try to accelerate, the car stalls in front of oncoming traffic. How would you feel? Terrified, no doubt! Not only are you in a dangerous situation, but the rules, as you know them, no longer apply. Life is not making any sense. Likely, you would ditch the car in a heartbeat. But what if you are stuck with this vehicle? You are forced to drive it every day. You try to tell others that the car is not working properly, but they blame your own driving ability. You take it to the mechanic, who says you are overreacting. How do you now learn to function? After driving the vehicle long enough, perhaps you find a way that works. It may be odd, but you latch on to anything that helps. If you need to roll down the window to get the turn signal to work, then you do it. What of young people with bipolar disorder who have lost the ability to manage their own emotions? At every turn there is a feeling of loss of control.

> "The idea free flow is fun and spurs on creativity, but sometimes I can't stop it. I feel out of control and I just want my brain to shut up." *Drew*

> "It can get annoying, because I can start to feel like it's out of my control. There is such a feeling of being too happy, when you can't control how talkative and hyper it makes you. I would feel overbearing and annoying to my friends." *Rory*

Young people with bipolar disorder grasp at anything in order to make sense of their world. It may make no sense to anyone else, but it helps them manage the unmanageable. With no control over their own emotions, they may pick something they can control, and hang on for dear life.

> "One thing that made me feel less irritable was being able to order my bedroom and keep it the way I liked. Going in my room and rearranging the furniture and neatening up made me feel less crazed." *Austin*

> "I learned to control hunger and not need food. I also worked to control my reaction to pain and discomfort by breathing and purposefully trying to slow my heartbeat. This was not relaxation, but control." *Dawn*

"I got bulimic because feeling like I didn't have any control became an issue. By having control over food, I allowed myself to believe I had some control over my life and my illness. I was also a cutter. It was something I did to help myself feel in control of my mind, which was going all over the place." *Drew*

Final Thoughts

Both Olivia and Jill compared the manic phase of bipolar disorder with a wave that goes higher and higher. Typical everyday waves are fueled by energy from the wind. But waves can also be created by energy released due to a catastrophic event, such as an underground earthquake or volcanic eruption. These are the waves that are most comparable to mania in children. The energy comes not from the winds of life, but from their illness. The resulting waves may start innocently enough, but the inevitability is that they will build into tidal wave proportions.

Surfers enjoy riding a high wave, and at times even put themselves in harm's way to feel the thrill that comes with it. The same is true with mania in the beginning. It may feel enjoyable in some ways to the young person. But at some point the wave becomes dangerous, threatening to overtake everything. The young person loses control as he is tossed to unmanageable heights. This type of wave can cause great devastation, and even loss of life.

Young people with bipolar disorder, unlike the surfer searching for a thrill, have no choice in the matter. They can't measure the weather and decide if it is safe to go into the water. These are children trapped on their surf boards, as it were. They can't trade in their boards or quit riding these waves as if this activity were merely a casual hobby. They are stuck with whatever the waves may bring, and they can only hope for a calm sea.

As with depression, the outward expression of mania is merely a part of what the young person experiences. While mania is quite different from its counterpart, it is no less impairing in both the inward experience and the outward manifestation. At this point we have discussed both "poles" in bipolar disorder: depression and mania. What of the transitioning between the poles? How does this occur, and how does the young person experience it? How do these contrasting realities affect the growing child? We will address these questions in our next section.

Section 3

Worlds Collide

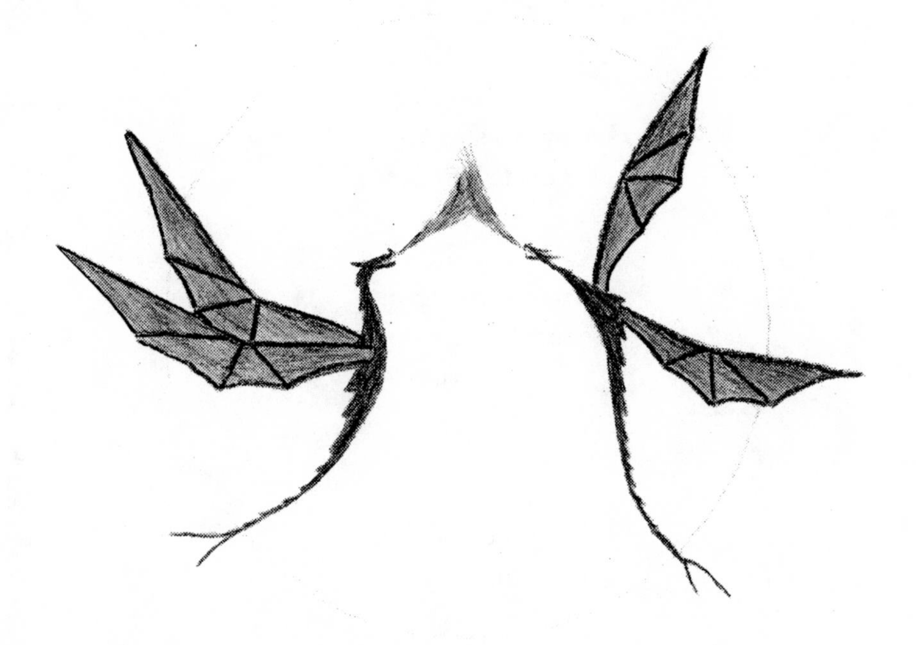

"Where have I gone?
What's the matter with me?
Why can't I just let me be?

Who is the real me?
Where does he go?
When I do something wrong,
He should know.

Why have I changed?
I'm not the real me.
Have I killed him?
Or made him flee?

I'm over here,
Please come again.
Look what I've done,
All this pain.

No one liked you,
I understand.
But I need you now,
Give me a hand.

I'm calling and screaming
With my mind.
All I need is to me find."

Todd Schwarz

The Wind Changes

My son charged through the front door, kicked at everything in his way, and stomped to his room. I tried to find out what was wrong. I asked if there had been a fight at the bus stop. He was so angry that his face was red and he couldn't speak to answer my question. Maybe something happened at school to set him off. I looked through his homework journal, searching for a note from one of his teachers. There was nothing. His teachers had not reported any incident. I quickly called the school, bracing myself for the bad news. What was the report I received? It had been a great day, with my son in a pleasant mood all day: no problems, no incidents and no conflict.

What a mystery. My son had left that morning in a good mood, had a great day at school, but was now in quite a different mood state. Eventually he calmed down enough to express his feelings. What had happened? The answer was nothing, at least nothing external. There were no fights at the bus stop and nothing that was particularly upsetting to him. On his walk home from the bus stop, he had been overtaken by a powerful change in emotion. There was no other explanation he could give for the mood shift, it just happened. In our family we refer to this as "the leaf falling." There is no warning. It can happen any time or place, without rhyme or reason.

> "The wind changes ... the mood shifts, and then comes the disillusionment." *Olivia*

Trading Places

Have you ever dreamed about switching lives or trading places with someone? It may seem appealing at first, but what if you had no choice? What if you were ripped from one identity to another, with no clue when it would happen or how long it would last? The result would be much uncertainty, confusion and anxiety. This is similar to the experience young people have as their mood states trade places. While there is always the existence of mania (or hypomania, which is a less severe form) and depression in bipolar disorder, it is the switching between these states that can largely determine the child's experience with his illness. The severity of symptoms in each mood state, the length of time he stays in the mood state, and the shift between the two states, all join together to create a young person's experience with bipolar disorder. This is why one young person with bipolar disorder may have a symptom presentation that is much different from another young person with the condition.

A young person who stays mostly in the depressed state, with few shifts into mania, will relate more closely to the feelings expressed in the first section of this book. This is the young person who may at first be misdiagnosed with unipolar depression. He may be given a treatment that only focuses on the depressed mood state, which has the potential to push him into the opposite extreme of mania.

A child who stays longer in the manic mood state, with few shifts into depression, will be able to relate strongly to the feelings found in the second section. A milder severity level may lead to a misdiagnosis of attention deficit with hyperactivity. Treatment focused on only this aspect of the experience may cause a worsening of symptoms, such as anger and irritability.

A child who cycles evenly between mood states will strongly relate to the feelings in each section. This is the young person who has a better chance of being properly identified. With proper identification there is a better chance of appropriate treatment.

These factors in how the young person shifts, or trades places, between mood states will influence both his experience with the illness and with the treatment of that illness. The speed with which these shifts happen will also have an effect. It is not uncommon for young people to shift mood states very rapidly, sometimes within a matter of minutes, making it difficult to even pick out the mood state. It should also be noted that a child can experience periods of wellness in-between these shifting moods. While this is a breath of fresh air, it is only a temporary reprieve from the extremes.

In all of the above scenarios, the child is pulled between extreme emotions. It's as if two opposite worlds are playing tug of war, with the child caught in the middle, hanging on for dear life. In some cases, the opposite sides of depression and mania seem to be equal in their strength and ability to drag the child back and forth. In other cases, one side seems to be winning, with the opposite side rallying occasionally to pull the child to its mood state. How does the shift in extreme emotions feel to the young person experiencing this phenomenon?

> "It feels like a ping pong ball going from one side to the other in my head – one bounce telling me to stay quiet, the other bounce telling me to scream." *Tim, age 15*

All Mixed Up

Along with this tug of war, which features both poles on the opposite extremes pulling the child back and forth between mood states, comes another unique mood state. It is called a "mixed state" and happens when the young person experiences symptoms of both depression and mania at the same time. It's as if the child playing tug of war has fallen into the muddy middle, which is a mixed up mess of the worst of both worlds. This is truly a very confusing state, but one that is frequently experienced by young people with bipolar disorder. Some spend most of their time in this state. They may crawl out of this middle muck to reach the edges of one of the mood states only to be sucked in, shot to the other side, and rolled back to the muddy middle.

> "It was a very dangerous time. I had bad thoughts and the energy to see them through." *Todd*

> "Nothing is worse than a depressed person with energy. Life is hopeless and bleak, but there's this urgency pressing at you to lash out at all the world's woes, whether outside or in. Or to be filled with a myriad of grand ideas, but you just can't get out of bed. The anger at yourself and your situation infects all those around you." *Dawn*

"I was happy and sad and angry all at the same time. I felt very alone." *Joan*

"I don't know if this is depression or mania or both, but whatever it was it didn't feel good. It was really, really horrible." *Bobbi*

Two Different Children?

A young person who falls into a consistent mood shift pattern may look and feel like two different children at different times of the day. Depending on which state is being experienced, the child may feel wonderful at school, with few difficulties, and a complete wreck at home. Or the opposite may be true. The young person may feel awful at school and wonderful at home.

One young woman relayed how her cycles flowed as a child. Quite often in the morning she would feel physically ill and depressed. She would have frequent school absences and tardees due to her difficult mornings. By evening, her energy level would increase. She would become very talkative and have pressured speech. Her parents would then conclude that she had been faking her illness in the morning just to get out of school. In actuality her bipolar disorder was cycling in a way that created difficulties for her morning activities.

Another woman shared with us her mood shift pattern

as a young person. It was just the opposite. This pattern in shifting resulted in better school performance and attendance, but a more difficult time at home.

> "I would try and get through the day in school and pretend that everything was OK, and by the end of the day I would just bomb and be relatively non-functional." *Drew*

External circumstances can also encourage the wind to blow, the leaf to fall, and a mood state to change. Each child may have specific triggers for this to happen, but there are a few that are common. Stress is a huge trigger for many children with bipolar disorder. Stress can actually worsen the course of the illness for a young person. Transitions and uncertainties, as well as parental separation, can be factors that cause the child an undue amount of stress, which can, in turn, trigger a switch.

Seasonal changes can also be a large trigger for mood states to change. So, along with experiencing daily or weekly emotional extremes, the young person may experience additional patterns of mood swings that last for months. An underlying depression may be stronger during the fall and winter months. The child may experience a stronger sense of mania in spring and summer.

"In retrospect, there were obvious periods of cycling, sometimes reaching hypomania and periods of depression, but normal periods were, at best, melancholic." *Gina*

"Fall was always a mood change time for me." Drew

"I experienced being slowed down in late fall to late winter a lot. I would basically withdraw into my own world, didn't want to do much but watch TV or listen to music in my room." *Joan*

"As it got closer to winter, I got more miserable and depressed. As the days became longer and sunnier, so did my disposition in general." *Tasha*

The Conflict

How do you come to know yourself? How do others come to know you as a person? We learn who we are through years of experience. Our consistent responses in various circumstances give us the information we need to define ourselves. These responses also give family and friends a sense of who we are as a person. Are you a shy person or outgoing? Are you mild tempered or easily roused to anger? Are you studious and responsible or careless and a poor performer? Are you friendly or surly?

Of course, all of us can be different in various settings or at different times, but we have a general concept of who we are as a person, our core being, and these differences fall within that concept. Consider the conflict and confusion experienced by the child who has no idea how he will feel or react in any given circumstance from one minute to the next. His entire reality becomes a conflict. Notice these opposing realities experienced by the young person, as exemplified in the following statements. Each conflicting statement is made by the same person describing opposite mood states.

> "Enthusiasm and involvement were big when I was up, so I joined lots of clubs, got elected to various student leadership roles, etc. As a senior in high school, I was the editor of the school newspaper, which I loved. I was competent at it and contributed a lot.
>
> Swing low and I was in big trouble; so much responsibility and no one there to do it. When I went low, I wouldn't even show up for class, dropping the responsibility entirely … for a while … until my mood switched up." *Olivia*

> "I was always outgoing and friendly. Life is so interesting and awesome.
>
> All of a sudden I felt dark and saw no importance in my life. I dropped out of cheerleading. I avoided my friends. I felt insecure for the first time in my life. I couldn't have cared less when I was depressed. I began skipping school just to be alone, which was really different than my normal, sociable self." *Miranda*

> "I have never been able to fall asleep. As a child I would stay up late into the night. I was concerned about my grades, and an overachiever. I aimed to please.
>
> I would sleep as much as I could and sometimes would not shower or take care of myself, just sleep. I didn't care what anyone thought because I just didn't care." *Drew*

"When I was manic agitated, I didn't sleep. I would just lie in bed and listen to my racing thoughts.

I wanted to sleep all the time when depressed. I would play alone. I was rarely happy and oftentimes irritable." *Dale*

"I had, for the most part, enjoyed going to school and doing family activities as a child. In school, I had lots of friends. I was a good student. I felt, at times, superhuman and able to take on more tasks at school. I would take on more homework, extra credit, join after-school clubs and over-commit myself to projects because I felt smarter than usual and more capable and excited to be doing tons of stuff at once.

When I crashed and fell into depression, I was no longer capable of fulfilling all these commitments. I stopped going to school. I stopped doing my homework. I stopped playing with friends and family. I couldn't get out of bed in the mornings." *Rory*

"I am an introvert normally.

I totally hid the manic stuff … being wild, drinking and being someone I wasn't." *Jordan*

"There were times that I could talk for hours on end, going from one subject to another.

It felt like I would be crashing down from a high because when it was over then I would be extremely quiet and almost felt tired and wanted to sleep." *Joan*

Who Am I?

Youth is a time we develop and define our identity. How do young people who experience the opposite poles that come with bipolar disorder view themselves? Just how do they come to grips with their confusing emotions? How do they begin to work through the conflicting experiences in order to define their being?

> "I remember standing in front of a mirror repeating out loud, 'You are Lee,' somehow, I guess, trying to find me in all the madness. I would get to the point that I would yell it into the mirror over and over, trying to figure out if there was a sane person there or if I was just some crazy person. I did this often in my manic phases." *Lee*

> "I used to look in the mirror and not really have the feeling of what was going on. I was just afraid." *Fran*

This is truly a confusing time. People who have a later onset of bipolar disorder may already have a clear mindset as to their identity, and thus see their mood symptoms as a clear departure from their normal experience. Young people whose onset was at a very early age don't have the advantage of developing their identity free of mood symptoms. Once they struggle to establish this identity, it is constantly being challenged.

> "Whatever was happening to me, I could not understand, nor could my family. I was unrecognizable to myself, and I hated myself for changing. I wanted to disappear. I felt like a failure." *Rory*

"I'm not sure who I am supposed to be! Which one is the 'real' person?" *Tasha*

"I felt like I was always an actor in character – getting good grades, being promiscuous – all of it was not me and felt weird. I had a major identity crisis; didn't know who I was or wanted to be. I also went through a very promiscuous time. It was not who I felt I really was, and it was humiliating to me." *Rachael*

Fears by Day

With all of these conflicting feelings and shifting mood states, it would be easy to understand that children with bipolar disorder experience a heightened degree of anxiety. However, it's not quite that simplistic. Anxiety is frequently one of the first symptoms to emerge in children who will go on to be diagnosed with bipolar disorder, so it is not necessarily a reactive emotion caused by this internal shifting. Anxiety is being recognized now as one of the markers for a young child who is at risk for developing bipolar disorder. While this anxiety may occur first, and be independent of shifting mood states, it also seems to be worsened by such cycling. Anxiety lies like a blanket over every mood state in bipolar disorder.

"I was scared about the world and fearful to do anything." *Joan*

"I remember going to a baseball game in the city as a child and sitting on the floor of the car because I was so afraid of being shot." *Olivia*

While anxiety can exist without outside influences, this symptom can be made much worse by stress and triggers specific to the child. This anxiety has physical effects on the child ranging from shaking and nausea to a full-blown panic attack, with racing heart, shallow breathing and chest pains. The young person experiencing these physical effects of anxiety may feel as if he is having a heart attack.

"I remember being quite anxious as a child. I would describe it as an unexpected event, where something normal would cause me to panic, my chest would tighten, my heart would beat rapidly and I would sometimes just break down and cry. It was very intense, and came on suddenly. It would take quite some time to settle down afterwards, and I felt very suspicious and paranoid until the episode would subside, which could be anywhere from 15 minutes to an hour." *Jan*

"It was third grade that I knew I would die in a vehicle accident at the age of 17. As I got a little older, I would make myself sick over anxiety of being in cars when it was raining or snowing. I would be so terrified that I would shake really bad and become nauseated. I would literally be in the back seat, praying. When I was 17, I stayed out of cars as much as possible. You can imagine the relief of my 18th birthday." *Grace*

"I would experience the sensation that my tongue was getting swollen and thick. I was scared to death." *Fran*

> "It feels like something bad is going to happen. Your stomach twists, you feel like running. You have shallow breathing. Your head feels weird, like something is unreal. There is this shivery feeling, for lack of a better word. I talk a lot and feel I have to find someone to take it away, which never happens. I get frantic. I feel like I have to hold something, like a stuffed animal." *Jill*

Lying in Dread

Nighttime can bring out some of these anxieties more intensely. Fears, in general, become stronger. Frequently, these fears focus around intruders, and deadly harm that might come upon the child or the household. These fears turn what should be a peaceful time into a traumatic experience. These young people with bipolar disorder lie in bed, frozen in fear and dread.

> "I'd be in bed at night and fearing for my life, for some unknown reason. I'd be terrified that someone was outside my window, a crazy maniac kidnapper who was going to get me. I just suffered in dead silence. I almost didn't even breathe. I felt that any movement on my part, including loud breathing, would make Him get me. If I heard an animal outside or the wind, I was convinced that He was getting tools out to cut my window screen, or something similar. I had vivid thoughts of what was happening and what would happen to me. I'd be in this state for hours, and it was extremely terrifying. I was convinced it was happening." *Jordan*

"When I was around 13 years old, at night I would think that I heard a loud ticking. The ticking would get louder and louder." *Fran*

"The fear was so intense for me; I would only lay on the inside of the bed by the wall and would only lay facing out. I was too afraid something bad would happen if I laid with my face toward the wall. I would also cry at night in bed with the fear that a plane was going to crash into our house, or that I wasn't going to wake up." *Carmen*

"I was an extremely anxious child, and afraid especially of war. If a Life Fight helicopter went over, I could not sleep. I was convinced we were having an air raid." *Drew*

"I remember having a hard time going to bed, because I was consumed with the idea of death. I was so afraid my parents were going to die. I would cry and cry, and my mother would try to help me. I was consumed with fear. I had to sleep with the windows shut even on the hottest nights. I would also always sleep with at least a sheet covering me. I wanted it to be extremely quiet, so I could hear any noises (people breaking in). I had to be ready." *Austin*

One would think that after lying in dread from all these possible threats that sleep would be a welcome peacefulness. But many young people with bipolar disorder are haunted even during their sleep.

Terror by Night

What is the worst dream you ever had? You probably remember it, even if you were a young child when you had the dream. The extremes experienced by youths with bipolar disorder don't spare their nighttime experiences. Their dreams are intense, and frequently marred by horrific images that are nearly unimaginable. There are no restraints in their dreams.

> "My dreams were scary. I was zipped in a bag of water in my closet drowning, while bad guys were killing my Daddy." *Steven, 11 yrs old*

> "I recall in detail my terrors. I don't think there is a word to describe what I 'saw.' I did not watch scary television shows or read scary books. In one gory night terror, my pet cat … my dearest possession, was brutally butchered and its parts were hanging from all different pieces of furniture in the living room. That image is, to this day, ingrained in my mind. Although it has been over ten years since I have had any terrors of any kind, I still have an extreme fear of the dark, and have a difficult time falling asleep." *Jan*

> "The night terrors were horrific. I can remember them back to about age 4. I would be scared to death to go to bed, and when they happened I would lay there frozen, waiting for the fear and anxiety to pass. The night terrors had an enormous impact on my self esteem. The night terrors made nights an anxious time, and it would carry over into the day, clouding experiences." *Olivia*

"I had, and have, horribly graphic night terrors. I have dreamed that I have been stabbed. I see my organs falling out of my stomach. I see the cuts and the blood. I feel the panic and fear. I hear the voice of my attacker, and I know there is no way out of it. Nothing helped, really. I felt I couldn't talk about it. Being undiagnosed, I had no idea what was wrong with me. Having all these morbid, horrible thoughts, I felt I was just going crazy. As a child, I just became more and more afraid, and more and more paranoid. I told no one of the monsters inside my mind." *Lee*

"I had nightmares a lot as a kid, and would oftentimes wake up screaming. Many of my bad dreams were of monsters killing my parents." *Dale*

"I have always had very vivid and many gory dreams. I see color and extreme detail. People come at me to hurt me, and I have this weird feeling like everyone is three times my size. I could see details, like if I shot someone in the head, then I could see the color of the blood and the blood spatter on whatever, and brains spatter on whatever. I could see the choke marks, and exactly what they looked like. It was like I was looking at point blank range in these nightmares." *Joan*

"Dreams were bad and scary. One was about this guy who would lock me in a room and throw rocks at me." *Brian, age 9*

These images seem so real at times that the child may have trouble distinguishing between dream and reality. The dream becomes an experience as if the child lived it. It is not surprising, then, that young people with bipolar disorder frequently sleep with the lights on, with their parents or siblings, and a trusted teddy bear. This comfort may be needed long past the usual age, and many times even into adulthood, due to the traumatic nature of their nighttime experience.

> "I think my dreams were more intensely real than other people's dreams. I often had trouble figuring out if something that happened in a dream was dreamed or really happening." *Tasha*

> "I did not sleep in my own room until I was nearly 13! I was absolutely terrified of the night. I had nightmares that were so vivid. I remember a repeat nightmare that a monster with huge teeth would come up behind me and bite my neck. I could see the blood trickle down and then pour out of the massive hole that was left. I would literally watch myself die! It was the same as living it! The fear of the night would put me into anxiety attacks." *Grace*

> "I experienced nightmares of such magnitude I'd awaken screaming and shaking." *Marty*

> "I would wake my younger sister and make her talk to me until I fell back to sleep." *Casey*

> "I recall very frightening and vivid dreams when I was a child and I would often scream out in terror. The only thing that would calm me down, so I could go back to sleep, was my father searching the entire house to show me there was no one hiding." *Alex*

> "My teddy bear tells the tale. He is so old and tattered. He was my anchor in many fierce storms." *Olivia*

> "My whole life, even now, I sleep with a stuffed animal." *Jill*

Don't Leave Me

This constant state of anxiety and fear adds to the children's already heightened emotional responses. They feel that there is a real threat to their life and well-being. Separation anxiety can be huge. During separation, children lose the protection of their parent(s). They also view the threat of danger to their parent as very real. Separation thus becomes a doubly difficult situation. Each separation brings the possibility that there will be no reuniting. They feel that through some horrific, unimaginable event, an event they have likely viewed over and over in their imagination or dreams, they will lose their parent in death, or their own life will be taken.

> "Those dreams would really affect me during my daytimes as well as the nighttime, in that I had a lot of separation anxiety. I was often fearful that, while I was at school, harm would come to my mom." *Dale*

> "As a young child, my fears of being separated from my mother in public were so bad. If I turned around and did not see her, I would get so upset I would vomit. I would look at another individual in a store and get severely anxious, thinking that man or woman was going to kidnap me or hurt my mother." *Grace*

> "Many adults scared me when I was not with my Mom or another adult I trusted. I used to fear school and feel bad when there. I felt unsafe if not with my Mom." *Jordan*

On the other extreme, the same heightened alert and anxiety that causes these young ones to cling to their parents also causes them to respond inappropriately to normal parenting or adult actions. Gina noted that children with bipolar disorder are very sensitive and have *an acute awareness of voice volume, a person's mannerisms, and tone.* A raised voice, corrective action or frustrated tone may be interpreted as a real, physical threat to their safety, even when coming from a trusted person. This perceived threat is very real to them, and may result in the young person taking defensive actions or lashing out against the threat.

Additional Challenges

At this point in your reading you may be saying, "Enough, already! These kids don't need any additional challenges." I agree with this sentiment. You will be happy to know that not all children with bipolar disorder have the following additional challenges. However, it is not uncommon for them to have additional challenges. What are some of these challenges? A specific symptom in bipolar disorder can be so pronounced that it merits a separate diagnosis altogether. For instance, a child may have an additional anxiety disorder or attention deficit hyperactivity disorder. Bipolar disorder also frequently co-occurs with other conditions that may not resemble any of the symptoms that are part of the illness. These all bring unique challenges to the young person already dealing with a difficult illness. Keep in mind that the brain is a complex organ and doesn't always fall neatly within the boundaries or categories assigned by people. Such categories do, however, help guide treatment. In view of the above it is not uncommon to see the following diagnoses along with bipolar disorder:

- Autistic Spectrum Disorders
- Tourettes and other Tic Disorders
- Obsessive Compulsive Disorder
- Attention Deficit Hyperactivity Disorder
- Anxiety Disorders
- Conduct Disorders
- Learning Disabilities
- Sensory Integration Dysfunction

While our focus is primarily on how it feels to grow up with bipolar disorder, any or all of the above conditions can have an impact on the child's individual experience. These may add a layer of complication and frustration. Taking all of these into consideration is important when trying to understand each child.

Final Thoughts

Olivia aptly described the unpredictability involved in switching mood states when she compared it to the wind changing. Winds can blow from any direction and change at any time without warning. They can blow softly or with hurricane force. Mood states are quite similar. They can change without warning and come on with full force or with deceiving subtlety. When they come on with the strongest of force, they can strike fear into your heart and turn your world upside down in an instant. Long after the winds have passed, you must deal with the destruction left behind, and the uncertainty of when the next strong wind will blow through.

Winds are also affected by outside influences, such as cold or warm fronts. The same is true of mood states. They can be triggered by outside sources also. For example, a switch in mood can be triggered by changing seasons and stress. There may also be individual triggers for each child that precipitates mood changes.

Now that you have an understanding of how the young person with bipolar disorder feels in specific mood states, and how these interact with each other, let's take this one step further. We are going to examine how the young person with bipolar disorder experiences the outside world. How does the illness effect interactions in school? How does it effect relationships with family and friends? How does the young person survive and cope? Is there anything good that comes from having bipolar disorder? And, is it possible to have a good life with bipolar disorder?

SECTION 4

Living

"I am unique, there's no one like me.
I see the world in its entirety.
I am special, something new.
I am strong, passionate, and true."

Todd Schwarz

Survival

One glance was all it took. I could see by their faces that something was wrong. The trip had not been a pleasant one. It was a short distance my son had traveled in the car. What had happened to make it a negative experience? It was a hot August day in Florida. My family was working on the property that would soon become our new home. My son was quite irritable, and the heat was making things worse. When he needed to find a bathroom, and none was readily available, a family member kindly offered to drive him to one. She tried to make pleasant conversation on the way, but what she got in return was a shockingly unpleasant response. My son angrily told her to be quiet and not to talk to him. They rode the rest of the way in silence, but the rift was obvious. On the way back, she corrected his manner of conversation and made clear that it was not appropriate to speak to her in that way. Fortunately, there were no permanent hard feelings.

This was a case of a young person with bipolar disorder knowing what he needed but not being able to convey that need in an acceptable way. He did need quiet at that point in time to deal with his own turmoil. He did alter his environment to get what he needed. However, he did not convey that need appropriately. The only way he could manage to convey his need was socially unacceptable, and came across as rude and disrespectful. But he did successfully get what he needed to survive at that point – quiet.

> "I was trying to survive in an environment that was not the same to me as it was to other people." *Tasha*

> "I was afraid of nothing due to having believed that I had experienced every feeling in the world. There was nothing left to hurt me. I did what I had to do to survive." *Linda*

Recognizing Needs

As humans, we have needs for certain things in life. We need food, water and clothing. We need love and friendships.

We need rewarding work and spiritual refreshment. Without these things our lives may be in jeopardy. Although we have some needs in common, we also have some needs specific to each person. Many times these needs are based on health concerns. People with diabetes have a need to restrict certain foods and to eat frequent, small meals. They must do this to maintain their health and stay in balance. People with asthma may have a need to avoid smoke or allergens that might trigger an attack. While these needs may limit the individual to some degree, failing to recognize the need could limit the individual even further and threaten his well-being.

Bipolar disorder is also an illness that comes with specific limiting factors. Recognizing these factors is vital to managing the illness and, ultimately, to survival and successful lives.

> "To do my homework, I would have to be in my room with the door closed and read out loud to myself. Reading out loud helped me concentrate and not get distracted with anything else going on in the house. My family used to HATE it." *Carmen*

> "I have a 'need' for certain things (quiet, calm, etc.) for day-to-day living. Sometimes the smallest tasks become impossible when there is too much noise or distractions." *Jan*

> "I would get so irritable with everyone that I wanted them to leave me alone." *Grace*

> "I am proud of how I have learned about my feelings and how to deal with them." *Mia, age 14*

Altering the Environment

When was the last time you altered your environment to make it more comfortable? You probably did today. Did you turn on the light to read this book? Did you turn on the heat or air conditioning in the car when you drove to work? Did you look at the caller ID and decide not to answer the phone because you didn't want to deal with the person on the other end?

Every day each of us alters our environment in a way that makes it more livable or comfortable. Sometimes these changes involve more than comfort and cross over into survival. For example, if you don't have heat in the middle of a blizzard, you could freeze to death. This alteration or manipulation of the natural environment becomes a way to survive. The same is true of young people with bipolar disorder. They must alter or manipulate their environment to meet their specific needs in order to survive.

> "Life means a lot of chaos. Grasping at coping strategies, constructive or otherwise, is all you can do. It reminds me of being out on a raft in the ocean riding the waves. All of a sudden a squall comes and the waves get really big and unpredictable. You are being tossed around and come crashing down only to be forced up again by the turbulent forces of the water. You have to

> do anything you can to stay connected and safe. You may cry, scream, try to swim, try to hold still and go with the swells, hold onto the raft for dear life, choose to let go of the raft and try to swim. You do whatever it takes to hold it together until the storm calms. It's survival." *Olivia*

While altering one's environment is actually an important coping skill, it is not viewed very positively in the world we live in. Being called a "manipulator" has a very negative connotation. The assumption is that the person manipulating things has a bad intent. This, of course, was not true of the person who turned on the air conditioner. There was no harm meant, only a change of environment. In the case of young people with bipolar disorder, manipulating their environment becomes a necessity to survive. That doesn't mean they always make the best choices on how to change the environment, but if one examines the situation closely, one will see the reason behind the manipulation.

> "I just felt not right and anxious and often felt ignored no matter how much attention adults tried to give me. Often the adults would end up thinking I was being manipulative or bratty. I used to fear school and feel bad when there and unsafe. I was feeling so bad I began to get physically sick, but my Mom and brother and teachers thought I was being manipulative. It was an awful time. One time, a teacher sent a note home when I was in about the fourth grade. It was not sealed, so I looked at it and it made me so embarrassed and ashamed. The letter was asking why I make things up, why I manipulate the school and her, and what is wrong with me to make me avoid school. I felt totally betrayed and humiliated. No one came to me EVER to ask why or what was wrong or do anything to help." *Jordan*

> "I would say I used manipulative ways in order to avoid school, because I had such a hard time being around others when I was depressed." *Miranda*

> "I definitely recall being manipulative, but for the most part, not out of spite. It was more of a protection mechanism when you felt threatened in some manner. It is a self defense mechanism of sorts." *Grace*

These manipulations, or *coping mechanisms*, do not end with youth. As young people grow and deal with changing environments, they must continue to find ways to alter those environments in order to function.

> "We are both (mother and son) spending our lifetimes trying to learn how to control the situations we are in, in order to better function in daily living. There are distractions that we are unable to block out of the background, therefore causing over-stimulation and eventual breakdown. We are trying to learn ways to handle the problem without creating friction in our relationships with others." *Jan*

> "In an effort to manage my situation in the workplace, I think others viewed me as manipulative. Honestly, it was a surrender, acceptance and effort to manage myself, stay employable, and regain my sanity and self worth. It was not until I implemented modifications that my quality and performance at work improved, and my temperament evened out." *Gina*

School

The school environment is a place of many challenges for the young person with bipolar disorder. It is a complex and demanding environment that mixes a tremendous amount of stimuli in with rigid demands of attention, concentration, social interaction and behavior. As we have seen from many experiences, bipolar disorder is an illness that affects energy levels, thoughts, moods and actions. Current research is showing that bipolar disorder impacts the area of cognition as well. Any one of these can have a strong influence on the young person's school experience.

Young people spend approximately 1,000 hours a year in school, making it a huge component of their lives. How, then, do the symptoms of bipolar disorder impact a child's functioning in school? What of the tiredness, heavy feeling and difficulty in making decisions? What of the emptiness, hopelessness and pain? What of the disconnection, guilt and anger? What of the racing thoughts and talkativeness? What of the increased energy and need to move? What of the crying, suicidal feelings and burden? The school experience for young people with bipolar disorder varies greatly, and is complicated by other things, such as learning disabilities and co-occurring conditions. However, there are some common experiences. First, let's consider some of these experiences in the depressive phase.

> "I had a lot going for me before I got sick. I was participating in post-secondary option, which allowed me to take college classes when I was young; ironically, I always thought I'd be a psychologist. When I became ill, I could barely stand to be at school. I felt that people were directing negative comments towards me. The reality was that no one understood what was happening to me." *Miranda*

> "I would go sort of on overload, and just couldn't think anymore. I think this was more defined when I was depressed." *Drew*

> "When I was in high school, I felt a lot of pressure to decide on what I wanted to do with my life and I just could not decide! I spent hours and hours looking at college and career information, and beating myself up mentally for not being able to commit to any course of action." *Tasha*

> "I never have been able to sit down for hours and study. I lose it after a half-hour at the most usually. I'm looking at the words, but have no clue what they say until reading the same paragraph at least three times. Indecisiveness killed me on tests. I could get absorbed in one question for twenty minutes on a multiple choice question, going between two answers." *Carmen*

> "I would take offense easily when I was at school. One day I was playing hopscotch with two other girls. When it was my turn I fell down, and both girls started to laugh. I started to cry and then started screaming at the top of my lungs, until all of the teachers came running to help me. I was hysterical as they took me into the school to call my mother. No one, including myself, knew why I reacted that way." *Alex*

"During the late winter I would become very tired. I would sleep all day on the weekends and would not want to get up to go anywhere. If I were at school or around a group of people while I was in this mood, I would grow very irritable and would not be able to sit still. It was more of an anger that would take over and cause my body to feel like it was going to explode." *Grace*

"If I couldn't be or do the best, then things became overwhelming. Even reading, which I love to do, became very difficult. The book seemed like it had too many pages, which would overwhelm me, so I gave up. I felt it was my sole duty and responsibility to attain some great understanding and insight into my homework assignment so that I could then enlighten and educate all of my peers. The fact that I could not accomplish this would send me into my downward spiral, contemplating my life once again." *Joan*

"Whatever I do must be the best, or otherwise I will avoid doing it at any expense. I felt I had to push myself all the time to please everyone. I remember vividly there was a biology test and there was a question I simply didn't know the answer for. I stayed and stayed in my desk while one student by one walked up to the teacher, handing in their tests. My face became red with embarrassment, but I was glued to my seat, struggling to answer that question. Finally, I chose the answer. To my dismay, it was not correct. All the other answers were correct, and as a result I got an A-, but I was so devastated that I was very down for the next few weeks." *Vivian*

"I started doing poorly in schooling. It was a struggle just to exist day to day. I remember one day, standing on a staircase in school, feeling bleak, hopeless and pathetic, just wanting to disappear from this Earth. I knew something had to change. I could not continue to live with these feelings." *Abbey*

> "I put immense pressure on myself to do well in school, and felt extreme guilt over this, even if I got an A- for a grade instead of an A." *Jordan*

Because much of depression is an internal experience, it is not always recognized by those around the child in the school environment. In many cases nobody seems to notice, and to the young person it feels like nobody cares. If it is recognized, it is sometimes attributed to other things, such as laziness. It is common for times of instability to be marked with frequent absences.

> "I would usually just lie in bed. I would tell my mother I felt sick and refuse to go to school. Not often did I miss school unless I was ill, but when this occurred, I would be ill for 2-4 days at a time." *Grace*

> "My second major depressive episode was at age 12 in the 7th grade. My depression hit me hard and swift. It was debilitating and unrecognized by anyone. During this period, having to go to school every day made it worse. I felt rejected and not liked. The symptoms of depression kept me from interacting with others on the same level I had been." *Bobbi*

> "I couldn't get out of bed for school in the morning, and when I did get up, I was miserable. I would skip school so I could sleep late. When I came home from school I would always take a nap. I had to sleep. I thought that other people found me worthless." *Austin*

> "I remember sitting on the back porch and watching the sun come up and trying to think of reasons to avoid school the next day." *Miranda*

> "Every year, from junior high through high school, I'd 'get sick' and be out of school for six weeks or more, usually in January and February. Then, the longer I was out, I'd get more and more scared about going back and facing the work that I'd fallen behind on! I'd be so scared that I'd actually shake and cry about it. By the time I'd 'recovered' and gone back to school, spring was coming." *Tasha*

As the young person switches to the manic state, the expression at school switches also. Remember, this switch may happen several times within the same day, or each mood could last longer periods of days or weeks. Some symptoms of mania may be mistaken for an attention disorder when displayed in the school setting. Racing thoughts prevent concentration and organization. Increased energy levels and talkativeness can be very disruptive to the classroom.

> "At school it was extremely difficult to organize thought and complete thoughts, ideas, projects and assignments due to the racing thoughts." *Lee*

> "I remember getting frustrated when someone read to me, because my mind would race so fast that I couldn't concentrate on the story. I would then reach a point that I would say I didn't care about the story anymore, holding back tears while I stomped off. I wished so much that I could be like the other kids and get the enjoyment they got out of it, but I somehow couldn't. I usually could not read and absorb the material. Either my mind would race or something would distract me, like a noise in the other room or something." *Jan*

"I often had trouble organizing my thoughts or focusing on specifics because my thoughts would just jump from here to there. When on the manic side, I was more of a clown and a talker. I remember, when I was 13 or so, I used to get in lots of trouble in English class. I love English and writing, but we would do this journal thing and I couldn't concentrate. I would talk with others and keep them from doing their work. Finally, the teacher put me in the hall for doing journal writing. Once I was away from all other distractions, it was easier to find a sense of focus." *Drew*

The anxiety associated with bipolar disorder can express itself in a variety of ways in the school setting. It can come in school avoidance, pressure to perform and be perfect, panic attacks, testing anxiety and social anxiety. It can be as impairing as any of the mood variations.

"I felt very anxious around others, especially new people. Sometimes, walking into a classroom with kids already in their seats would cause me anxiety, because I had to walk in front of them." *Joan*

"I literally did not speak one word to my kindergarten through second grade teachers. I remember many trying to bribe me with candy to get me to speak. I kind of resented those attempts. It felt as if I wasn't good enough just the way I was, and that I was being punished for being me when I wasn't given the treat. In third grade, I was sent to a different school district, and this seemed to give me a new start somehow, as I began to speak to my teachers when necessary." *Jan*

"I had a complete fear of going to school. I would leave the house and hide in the woods until darkness." *Mark*

"I can remember nearly every day on the bus I would get so nervous, just knowing that it would roll over, and everyone, especially me, would die a very painful and gruesome death. I would even picture my mother seeing me dead like that, and those visions were so real." *Grace*

"I had a lot of social anxiety, which for me goes along with depression. I felt completely alone and I hated school after this." *Bobbi*

"Probably the worst thing for me in kindergarten was the air raid drills we had to do. I remember crying uncontrollably and sitting in the hall. I still have panic attacks when I hear certain alarms go off." *Carmen*

"I was very embarrassed to eat in front of others, so I would eat in another room at home. At school I would not eat at all, for fear of someone making fun of me. Clattering forks and spoons set me off, or the sound of a fork hitting someone's teeth. The sound of someone eating was like a trigger. I just wanted to yell, 'Stop! Shut your mouth!' Sounds, to me, are very disturbing and put me on edge quickly." *Lee*

"I think that anxiety was the worst part of it. In school it would start with a long night of test prep, up early in the a.m. to review, and then a knot in my stomach so tight that when it reached my head, my thoughts and ideas were a whirlwind. I could not pull a clear thought out. It was a cell that locked from the inside." *Gina*

In the section titled Worlds Collide we discussed the fact that young people with bipolar disorder can experience their illness in a variety of ways. Their experience depends greatly on how they switch mood states, how long they stay in each state, their degree of impairment, and what additional challenges they may have. These factors also mix together to make up the child's school experience. Some children with bipolar disorder are so impaired that they have to attend a therapeutic school setting. Others are less impaired and able to expend an enormous amount of energy to hold themselves together during school, or cover over their emotional turmoil. This, however, usually comes with a large price, as the emotions can only be contained for so long before they spill over.

> "I was able to hold it together in school and actually got very good grades." *Casey*

The child's functioning may be quite different from day to day, week to week, month to month and year to year. If this is difficult for the child to comprehend, and for adults to comprehend, think of how it confuses peers at school and interferes with social interaction. Young people with bipolar disorder may be especially susceptible to bullying. They frequently have difficulty making and keeping friends.

> "I don't feel like the other kids at school. I feel like I'm left out. I want to be like a normal kid. I go in the tunnel on the playground at recess so I can think about how to help myself, because I feel like crying during recess when people say mean things to me like, 'You aren't very smart.'" *Alisha, age 7*

"I was ostracized by my friends for not going to school." *Rory*

"Kids fight a lot, and there is always someone bullying me or calling me names. I have tried to use the mediation system, but it doesn't help. They go back on their word." *Steven, age 11*

"I didn't belong to any particular group. I was a loner, somewhat accepted by everyone, but belonging nowhere." *Ashley*

"I really only had one friend in school. I remember spending many days at recess by myself." *Carmen*

Without the proper education regarding bipolar disorder in young people, a teacher might inadvertently worsen an already bad situation. A caring, understanding teacher can make a world of difference for a young person with bipolar disorder. They can inspire, encourage and truly be a favorable influence. Conversely, a harsh and critical teacher can feed into the child's instability, and leave scars that last a lifetime.

"In first grade I often got my mouth taped shut because I talked too much. I spent a lot of time in the corner. The teacher yelled at me so much I developed a slurring of my speech, and I was afraid of teachers." *Jill*

"Not only would I talk a lot, but I would be very 'giddy.' I would laugh for no reason and not be able to stop. In second grade, I had a teacher who humiliated me for talking. One day she screamed at me and moved my desk to the front of the room. I was crying hysterically and felt REALLY humiliated, bad about myself, and embarrassed." *Carmen*

"I do not like school. The teachers make it worse. They keep on piling it on when I can't think. I go to the bathroom to get away. The teachers don't seem to care or understand me and they don't pay attention to the teasing that goes on until it is out of control. I hate to go." *Steven, age 11*

"I don't like school because they treat me like a baby. My classes are my worst part because they treat me like I'm stupid. When I have trouble, they tell me I'm being lazy and don't really want to learn, like I'm trying to fool everyone. My teachers don't help me when I have a bad day. They ignore me, or send me out of class to time-out to sit, instead of finding out why I'm having a bad day." *James*

Family

Any family who has a child suffering with a chronic illness can attest to the difficulties of family life. There is both economic and emotional strain when medical difficulties arise. Like any child, a young person with bipolar disorder may have loving, caring parents or a dysfunctional family. Either way, his illness will interfere with family interaction. The symptoms of this illness can take the entire family on an emotional roller coaster ride. If these symptoms are left unidentified, they may baffle and confuse parents and siblings. Even when the illness is identified, disappointments, concerns, arguments and frustrations are all common. In the worst situations, ignorance causes a poor response which could ultimately destroy relationships and push the child further into depression.

"My mother didn't know what to do with me." *Dale*

"My parents thought I was becoming lazy and didn't care about myself, but the truth was that I didn't know what was happening to me." *Joan*

"I remember a lot of dark days, just wandering around, not happy with anything, irritable, and always fighting with my mother. No matter what she said, I would say the opposite. I always felt unsettled inside, not being able to concentrate on anything at home." *Casey*

"My family and friends watched as I withdrew from my life and lost my spunky, positive personality. My family, though supportive and active in my recovery, watched me pick at my dinner with tears streaming down my face. I found it hard to communicate." *Miranda*

"I was told how retarded, demonized and horrible a child I was. So I never felt I was wonderful or good." *Dawn*

"Something would set me off crying and I wanted to stop but couldn't. My family tried to comfort me, but could not. They didn't understand me, but I couldn't understand me either. Being with or around my family made my depression worse, because they thought I was overacting or being dramatic or playing the victim. All I wanted to do was curl up and die. They never saw this, or even began to grasp it." *Rory*

"I saw my family situation, and my world, as a place that I didn't fit in. I didn't feel that my parents loved me." *Fran*

> "I was often suicidal. My mom would say, 'Let me get a knife for you.' That would make it worse. My parents had no clue as to what was wrong with me. My mother, being the only witness to my rages and major mood swings, would only scream, slap or ignore me. This would fuel them. My sister, loving me anyway, would help. She would come in and sneak me dinner when I had put everyone, including her, through hell. She had a silly sense of humor, and she wouldn't stop, no matter how depressed I was. She wouldn't stop until I had laughed. She wrote me notes saying she loved me anyway. My dad did the same." *Lee*

One of our participants expressed a view held by many when she lamented the effect her illness has on others. There is no joy for the young person that her condition makes family life difficult, nor is there control to change this fact.

> "If I could change one aspect of bp, and I would like to change many, it would be for the cycles to have no impact on others. It's one thing to have to endure the inconsistencies within oneself. That's really hard. But to affect others with all of the unpredictability just doesn't seem right." *Olivia*

Friends

How do you pick your friends? Are they similar to you or different in personality? No matter what attracts you to another person, your friendship is based on knowing who that person is. What if you have a sense of who a person is but then he is constantly changing? He seems quiet and shy, but then, all of a sudden, he is talkative and outgoing. Or perhaps he is funny and exciting, but changes to being withdrawn and sullen. Worse yet, maybe he is irritable, cranky and argumentative. You can imagine the difficulties this would pose in maintaining friendships.

> "I can recall times of being around friends that I grew up with, and they would come from the city to play. I would tell them all sorts of things of how I was so cool. I would say things that made me look to be better than anyone else, and to heck with anyone who thought otherwise. I could do anything and I could be anything, and was the best at it. I lost some of my friends over this. Other times, I would close my shades all the way and would not accept calls from friends, and would not go to the door if they came to my house to play." *Grace*

> "I was trying to please the people around me because I felt so insignificant, and I thought if people liked me, it would give me a redeeming quality, and perhaps a reason to live. I have friends get frustrated with me (when manic and over-talkative) because I don't make a lot of sense to them and I am just turning them in circles." *Drew*

> "My parents had to pick me up in the middle of the night during some of my sleepovers because I would keep screaming (due to a nightmare) even after I awoke. This made it even more difficult for me to keep friends, as I would feel ashamed and would withdraw even more into myself. It was difficult for me to make and keep friends." *Marty*

> "Sometimes an issue with friendships is that the connection is stronger with others when you talk a lot. This would strengthen a friendship that might have been less significant to me. They

feel they get a sense of who I am. Then my mood will switch, and they become baffled and disillusioned, confused actually. I am basically the same person but less reliable, or less trustworthy, or less motivated than they thought I was. The opposite happens as well. They feel they get a sense of who I am. Then my mood will switch and they become amazed at how engaging and capable I am." *Olivia*

"I was always argumentative about my side of everything and felt the other person should realize that I was right. I felt like I had all the answers. I was bossy to most of my friends, wanting things my way. I felt my happiness should be very important to everyone else, even if it meant others weren't." *Joan*

Take Away the Pain

When we are sick, we usually look for ways to feel better. Walk into any pharmacy and you will see an array of remedies targeted at reducing pain. Whether we use totally natural products or synthetic ones, pain drives us to look for a remedy. Young people with bipolar disorder are no different. If their pain is not identified and treated, they will search for relief. They try to escape the anguish, quiet their mind and kill the pain. Unfortunately, this makes them very vulnerable, and can lead them to experiment with drugs and alcohol. There is a high risk of substance abuse with mood disorders. Alcoholism and drug use in the family tree is a marker that may indicate a mood disorder.

"When I got into high school, drinking became an issue and problem for me." *Joan*

"I got into drugs, alcohol and sex to kill the pain." *Tasha*

"I started self medicating probably around 17 years old. It must have helped for the moment because I continued for years. I was obsessed about having some kind of drug, because being me was not comfortable. I also spiraled into bulimia and anorexia by late teens." *Gina*

"Sometimes, during these periods, I would self medicate with alcohol or pot." *Mark*

"I am ashamed to admit that for a year or so before I was diagnosed as bipolar I took a destructive road towards drugs and alcohol. I tried using marijuana to mellow me out. It wasn't helpful." *Miranda*

"As a teen the depression got worse. I then got involved in alcohol. I was drinking every day after school, not to get drunk but to just escape this world. I just wanted to be dead. I didn't really ever think of recourse or consequences." *Linda*

"I started drinking at age 13. I began hanging around with a different crowd and drinking and doing drugs." *Bobbi*

"I dabbled in mild drug use and alcohol use at this time, and that made things worse." *Drew*

"Eventually, I began to drink and take pills to calm my sense of sadness and depression, as well as to calm the 'crazies." *Fran*

The Twist

Are you ready to hear the good news yet? After reading thus far, you may wonder if there is any good news about bipolar disorder. I'm happy to say that there is. Your understanding of youth with bipolar disorder would be sorely incomplete if you did not recognize some of their amazing gifts and the good things that come with this illness. Some of the most gifted, intelligent, creative, intuitive, and artistic people have bipolar disorder. Many young people with bipolar disorder have a unique perspective on life. They may also go on to learn things from their illness that benefit them in their adult lives.

> "It has forced me to reevaluate my values, perceptions, convictions, and has enabled me to become more of an active humanitarian in my later years." *Marty*

> "I feel and believe that there are many good things that I have gained from this illness. I have the ability to tap into really creative channels and think outside the box. I also feel that having such an acute illness, and having grown up with it, allowed me to be empathetic with others in all areas of life." *Drew*

> "I am more in tune with my emotions than many, and this can help in being creative too." *Joan*

"The manias make you very determined. I always found a way to make things happen. Bipolar gave me the opportunity to help others in ways that many people will never be able to. Even as a kid I would cry with my friends because I felt their pain. I also have helped many whose lives have also been affected by this illness." *Grace*

"I was so often told I was visionary, creative and gifted. I have a contentment and happiness that I often see others missing in their lives. For example, I will see a child in McDonald's spill a drink on his mother's dress, and she will 'hit the roof,' so to speak. I've hit rock bottom, and know that a spill on my dress is no comparison. I have learned to take every waking moment as the best it has to offer. I try to do something enjoyable, no matter how small, every single day. Another quality I have noticed is a greater sensitivity, compassion and acceptance of others. I have learned to have an appreciation for the good things that I received in my mother's womb, and temporarily grieve the bad things. This has certainly given me a different perspective, appreciation and/or patience with other people's talents, gifts or lack of them. For this, I am thankful. I've learned that I am not valuable because of my potential, rather I am valuable because I exist." *Jan*

"I use the illness to my advantage. Be strong and remember where you have been and what you have been through. If I beat those days, I can beat anything now that I know the illness, the symptoms and the feelings of it." *Linda*

"The best thing about learning that I was bipolar was that I finally understood this 'thing' that haunted my family. After learning as much as possible about bp, it helped me to understand my mother's suicide." *Alex*

"The ups and downs can be difficult, but I love being creative." *Mia, age 14*

"Through it all, I have become a stronger, more sympathetic person. I am very compassionate to others, and I believe that is because of the obstacles I've overcome due to bipolar disorder. Yes, my illness can be devastating, but there are times when I am so happy and appreciative of life because I have made it from the bottom to the top." *Miranda*

"I am certainly more understanding about people with mental illness, more compassionate. I have been able to fight for my daughter who has bipolar, because I knew early on that something was wrong. I can advocate for her, because I understand when nobody else does. I can be very creative at times, and my mind is always thinking. I won't settle for just existing in life. Bp has given me the creativity and drive to do some really cool things. It has also given me great insight into myself. I've learned what bothers me, what I can tolerate, what annoys me and gets me agitated. Through this, I have learned how to deal, not only with myself, but with others as well. I have learned how to say the things I need. I can say to my husband, 'I need some time alone. There is too much activity.' This has helped me in all areas of life." *Austin*

"I am a very social person, and have the ability to empathize with anyone. I'm a shoulder for my friends, and I think it's because I've been through a lot that I can understand almost anything others go through. I'm very outgoing, and it has helped me in my jobs, as I've always worked with the public. I no longer fear what others think about me. I know my own experiences make it easier for me to understand what my son must be going through now. I can see the child he really is, as opposed to the illness that he's fighting. I can appreciate his assets and his gifts, so it's a bit easier to get through the tough times. I think it was easier to accept his diagnosis." *Tasha*

"I have a very strange sense of humor, very offbeat. I can make people laugh. I hear, 'Only you, Lee!' at least twice a week, along with rolling laughter. That makes me happy even if it's a day that I'm feeling like I want to fall apart. At least I made someone else happy." *Lee*

"So many good things have come from my being bipolar. Life has been anything but bland. I think the hypomania allowed me to get two master's degrees. I remember writing 10-15 page papers in grad school practically at one sitting. I have made many friends due to the fun, outgoing side of hypomania. I think being bp makes me more sensitive to others. I care about the feelings of others, and can connect with all kinds of people. It also helps me understand my son. His world is very complex. It's tiring as a parent to respond to it every day, throughout the day, when they are symptomatic … and, yet, when I look at it from my son's point of view, I feel very sympathetic. It's really tough on him. Sometimes, when I get frustrated with all of his neediness, I can imagine myself as a little girl suffering, and my compassion overrides my frustration." *Olivia*

"When in a manic mode a lot gets accomplished. I feel being bipolar has helped me deal with my mother and sister, who are also bipolar. As a mother in dealing with my two bipolar children, it has helped me a great deal. I am more tuned in to what my kids are saying, where they are coming from, and on the same wavelength, so to speak. As a nurse, I think I have been able to relate to people and help them more." *Carmen*

"I have known pleasure in life that others cannot imagine. I have been in such depths of depression and anxiety that I can relate to anyone who struggles with similar problems. I have supported those with mental illness with my time and resources. I understand my bp children, and I want them to be parented differently than I was parented. Had I not been hyper focused, I would have never made it through nursing school. It's been a curse and a blessing, but I would not be the person I am now had I not had to work so hard to get here. I love the simple things:

birds, flowers, children, family. New day, new hope, new joy!"
Gina

Final Thoughts

Both Tasha and Linda talked about the need to survive. People who are in situations that threaten their very existence go to extremes in order to preserve their lives. A case in point is the experience of a hiker whose arm was pinned under a boulder. After being pinned for five days in a remote canyon in Utah, the 27-year-old man performed his own amputation in order to survive and reach safety. Another man, whose leg was pinned under two boulders, also made this drastic decision to save his life. These examples indicate that the human instinct for survival is strong. While these are extreme cases, they have something in common. In both instances, the men involved felt that their lives were in jeopardy, and they did what they had to do in order to survive.

Bipolar disorder is an illness that threatens life. Most of us don't consider day-to-day living as survival, but for young people with bipolar disorder, that is exactly what it is. Growing up with bipolar disorder is exceedingly difficult. Both school and home environments are strongly affected, and also influence the young person. Living becomes a matter of survival, and altering one's environment becomes an important part of that survival.

We also see that these young people may be kissed with artistic talent, unique intellect and a drive to accomplish great things. Their survival helps them mature and grow in ways that make them highly compassionate and appreciative of beauty in simple things.

Our picture of bipolar disorder in young people is now complete. Hopefully, both your understanding and compassion have been deepened through this journey. If you are one who has experienced these intense emotions first hand, it is hoped that you feel comforted and validated by the recognition and acceptance of your symptoms and their effects. There is, however, one thing left for us to understand. Perhaps it is the greatest of all. How do you fit into this picture? What is your role? How can you reach out and help? Whether you are a teacher, a parent or a medical professional, you can make a difference. Let's find out how.

Section 5

Making a Difference

"I understand,
I'm here, I care.

You can open to me,
If you dare.

Because when you're down,
I'll be there.

With warm whispers,
Letting you know I care.

For only you,
My long lost loving one,

I'll be your comfort,
'Till your pain is done."

Todd Schwarz

Plea for Help

My son saw a developmental pediatrician when he was about 10 years old. She asked him what he would wish for if he had three wishes to spend. His first wish was that he would no longer have bipolar disorder. If I could make that wish come true for him, I would do it in a heartbeat. I can't. But that doesn't mean I am powerless. Before we learn more about what we can do, let's listen to the wishes of others who grew up with bipolar disorder.

> "I ***wish*** someone had realized I was depressed. It would have helped. But no one did, or at least no one tried to help if they did." *Jordan*

"I think I would have been MUCH better off had I been diagnosed as a kid. The illness still would have remained a part of my life, but I probably wouldn't have gotten as ill. When I think of all of the hours of peace it might have replaced in my childhood, it makes me ***wish*** that I had a chance for recovery then." *Olivia*

"I turned to drugs and alcohol to treat the symptoms of bp. Drugs and alcohol nearly killed me. I wasted a lot of time being depressed and sleeping. I ***wish*** I could take that back." *Austin*

"I think I would have been better off as a child if I had been diagnosed and medicated. I wouldn't have suffered so much depression and gone through so many destructive relationships. I may have been able to enjoy my teenage years more. It really makes you ***wish*** you could go back and do it over with the knowledge and self esteem you have now." *Casey*

"The medications helped tremendously and ended the hallucinations quickly. I just ***wish*** that in the beginning the doctors didn't put me on so much medicine. I think that trying one or two at a time would be more effective. I just know that the medications had a lot of side effects. Today, my lithium doesn't even affect me at all. The dosage is perfect, and I can continue to be active and participate in activities that I love." *Miranda*

"The struggle of being depressed at a young age is huge, and I wanted someone to notice my struggle and tell me what was wrong with me. I think I would have been better off if I had been properly diagnosed earlier on. I was incorrectly diagnosed and, therefore, incorrectly medicated, which made my bipolar symptoms worse, and even sent me into manias. I ***wish*** that people such as teachers, and even doctors, would have had more information, because then perhaps I would not have had to suffer for so long. If I had kids, I would be aggressive in seeking diagnosis and medication, because by prolonging it I know that it would be harder on my child and my family. Mental illness sucks, but with proper diagnosis and treatment, life can be relatively manageable." *Drew*

"I don't want anyone to go through the horrors I have had to go through." *Mark*

"I think knowing earlier and being treated would have kept me from self medicating, sleeping around, and maybe even saved my marriage. Understanding and education can fix a lot of things." *Tasha*

What Parents Can Do

The parent or any primary caregiver of a young person with bipolar disorder has an extremely important role. The responsibility for getting your child the help he needs falls on your shoulders. It is likely that you are the first one to notice the symptoms of bipolar disorder as they emerge. If you are just beginning this journey and are unsure if your child is suffering from bipolar disorder, the first step is to take him to his pediatrician for a complete physical. It is important to rule out other medical conditions that can mimic the symptoms of bipolar disorder. A complete exam, blood work, and possibly further testing may be performed. If symptoms persist, then it is important for you to seek out more help for your child.

In order for a young person with bipolar disorder to successfully navigate into adulthood, it is vital for him to have a team of people assisting him. As a parent, it is your job to build that supportive team. You are the "leader" of the team, so to speak. Who should you choose to join you on your child's team? These are important decisions, as the right professionals can make a huge difference in the outcome of treatment.

The most important choice you will likely make is the child's psychiatrist. You may first have to battle your own misconceptions about the field of psychiatry. If your child had a problem with his heart, would you hesitate to take him to a cardiologist? While it might be scary to deal with the illness, you would likely want the first appointment available. So why do parents sometimes get squeamish about taking their child to a psychiatrist? Mostly due to the stigma that is promoted by society. That is unfortunate. So, let's set the record straight. A psychiatrist is a medical doctor. He or she must graduate from college, then medical school, and spend four years in a residency program in the field of psychiatry. If the doctor is a child psychiatrist, then she has also completed additional training in this area. It is advisable to find a child psychiatrist who is experienced in treating pediatric bipolar disorder.

How do you go about finding the right doctor? You can check with local mental health advocacy groups. While they may not be able to give you a direct recommendation, you can network with other families in your area. They can likely give you a lot of good information about the quality of care in your area. Another excellent resource in finding professionals who frequently treat bipolar disorder in children is the "Find a Doctor" listing at the Child & Adolescent Bipolar Foundation (CABF). This is available 24 hours a day online at www.bpkids.org. You will also want to visit the Juvenile Bipolar Research Foundation at www.jbrf.org, where you can download screening tools and a questionnaire for your child. This can help you communicate your child's current symptoms to your health care professionals.

While these first steps are difficult, remember that you are doing something incredibly important for your child. It may, indeed, be the best gift you can ever give him or her. It is not a sign of weakness, but a sign of strength and love.

> "I hope that most parents can identify the level of suffering the child is experiencing. Everyone within the family structure is suffering, but the child who is symptomatic needs a triage approach. Drop life as much as possible to work with doctors, med trials, school, family, etc. It's a wild ride, but you're strapped in and it's taking off, so you might as well learn how to hold on and keep everybody safe." *Olivia*

> "I do seek help for my kids. I don't care about the 'labels' others may be worried about, because my children's mental and physical health are just too important. This is about their quality of life. They deserve, and have a right to, the best we can give them. My life has been through hell and back, and I didn't know what was happening to me until my diagnosis." *Joan*

> "With being a nurse and having two children that are bp, there is just no question about treatment. My kids were definitely diagnosed and are on medication. Why should they suffer in ways I did from not being diagnosed? Suffering with this beast is bad enough. I wouldn't be taking care of them if I didn't. It is my job as a mother to help them grow and to nurture them so they can develop into happy, healthy, functioning adults, something that didn't happen for me." *Carmen*

> "Understanding the crucial effect that bipolar disorder can have on one's life, I insisted on having my child, who has bipolar, properly diagnosed and put on medication that is specifically for bipolar disorder." *Jan*

In addition to the child psychiatrist and the primary caregivers, there are others who will be on the child's support team. Hopefully this will include other supportive family members, but don't be surprised if this doesn't happen right away. They may be battling their own fears and misconceptions. A young person attending school will need team members who are part of the school environment. As time goes on there will be various school personnel involved in your child's support team. Because school is such a big part of the day for young people, it is important to work together. Your first instinct may be to hide your child's illness from the outside world. Again, this is a result of stigma, and does not serve the best interests of the child. While you don't have to shout private medical information from the rooftops, you do need to share such important medical information with those working with your child. To learn more about advocating for your child at school, visit the STARFISH Advocacy Association online at www.starfishadvocacy.org.

Any parent of a chronically ill child can testify that there is a grieving process that occurs when a child is diagnosed. While you may have known in your heart that there was something wrong, hearing it for the first time can be devastating. Allow yourself time to grieve, and don't be surprised if your grief revisits you when your child's symptoms worsen or when you see your child struggling to reach important milestones while others of that age group are sailing through them. Surround yourself with support. You are not alone. Some doctors estimate that there are nearly a million children in the United States who have bipolar disorder. That means there are a lot of parents out there in the same boat. Find them through support organizations. Surround yourself with people who care. You can find support organizations by referring to Appendix A in this book. Most of them have a Web site where you can search for local chapters. Additionally, there are some that feature online support groups.

> "I have been stable for four years now, with much relief from my family and friends. Education has been the key to my well-being. My mother attended NAMI meetings to understand my symptoms, and we finally began seeing a light at the end of the tunnel. I remember my mom saying, 'You'd be there for me, right?' And I guess she was right. Getting treatment for mental

illness is tough, and I couldn't have done it without the support and love from my family." *Miranda*

If you are not new to this road, but instead you are an old-timer who probably should go ahead and get your degree in psychopharmacology, beware of caregiver fatigue! It can creep up on you just when you feel like you have everything under control. Both parents of newly diagnosed children and those who've been around the block need respite. If you don't take care of yourself, you will not have the energy to take care of your child. This is not a sprint, but a marathon run that requires stamina.

As time goes by there will likely be additional mysteries that come up. Bipolar disorder frequently comes with co-occurring conditions. Getting to the bottom of these may mean the difference between stability and instability. For instance, some children achieve a certain degree of stability with treatment, but then still have residual symptoms. They may have learning disabilities, sleep problems, sensory integration issues, and so forth. Left unaddressed, these can interfere with a child's recovery. As the primary caregiver, you are the one who sees your child's frustrations. It's important to report these to the treating physician. Be open to the idea that you may have to include even more professionals on your child's team. Some of these may include a neurologist, developmental pediatrician, occupational therapist, psychologist, endocrinologist, etc. After a while you may feel that your child has seen every specialist in the book, but each doctor may contribute to one more level of stability and help uncover other health issues that may be overlooked initially when the priority is on the safety and stabilization of the child.

Young people with bipolar disorder are very complicated. I compare them to "Shrek," the ogre in a popular children's movie. It's not that I think my son is an ogre, but in this popular children's movie Shrek refers to himself as an "onion," meaning that he has a lot of "layers." I think of my children as having layers of need. As you address and peel each layer back, you can see more clearly what the next layer is, and how to address it. Dealing with each layer of difficulty contributes to their success. Why should you make the effort to search through each difficulty? Because hiding in the middle are an incomparable beauty and a strong spirit waiting to be nurtured and released.

This is all fine and good, you may think, but how in the world do I deal with the difficult manifestation of this illness during times of instability? This is the million dollar question. While there is no magic solution, beginning with a base of understanding is important. This is an illness, and adaptations are going to have to be made. Reducing stress is vital as the child tries to stabilize. You may have to adjust your thinking and expectations. Your child can still be successful, but he may not always be able to function in the capacity you had previously hoped or in a way that is commonly accepted by society. Working with a therapist may help you figure out the best way to deal with family situations. If your child is explosive in nature you will want to read The Explosive Child by Dr. Ross Greene. This will give you concrete ways to handle a difficult child while you try to help him towards recovery. There are several other helpful books, including The Bipolar Child by Dr. Demitri F. Papolos, M.D. and Janice Papolos, which you will want to read as you progress on your journey. You will find these valuable aides listed in Appendix B.

Right now your child needs to know that you love and care for him, and that you are here to help. You can answer the plea of your own children by developing a treatment team for them, not letting stigma stand in your way. See not just their symptoms, but the suffering underneath, and address this with the understanding, love and the kindness you would want if you were in your child's position.

> "I craved so much for someone to just look at me with a smiling face and say, 'I love you for who you are.' And if someone did, which was very rare as people were very uncomfortable to be around such a sad girl, I soared into the sky like a free eagle. I would beam very brightly but, like the flame of a candle, it did not last." *Vivian*

What Health Practitioners Can Do

Some months after my son began treatment for bipolar disorder we ran into a snag. We had seen improvements in my son's mood swings, and he was feeling better. Even so, he did not like to take the medication that his psychiatrist had prescribed. It soon became a daily battle. At his next visit with the doctor, I informed him of my child's reluctance to take medication for his illness. I sat back, fully expecting the doctor to give my child a lecture on the necessity of taking medication. By my son's demeanor, he was probably expecting the same thing. To my surprise, the doctor did nothing of the sort. Placing his elbows on his knees with his hands clasped in front of him, the doctor leaned forward in his chair so that he was looking right into the eyes of my son. He said, "I know it's no fun to take medicine. How can I make this easier for you? What can I do to help?" My son had no ideas, but his attention was totally engaged. The doctor continued. "Would it help if you could take your medication with a favorite drink? What do you like?" Now my son smiled. Yes, he agreed, it would be much easier to take his medicine if he could drink something special with it. The issue was settled, and I stopped on the way home to pick up his favorite drink. I learned an important lesson that day: human compassion is one of the greatest tools a doctor has.

While this may seem like a small matter, it was not small to my son. It was important to him. His doctor listened, got on his level, engaged him in the solution, showed empathy and concern, and helped him be compliant all at the same time. What an example for practitioners everywhere. We talked earlier about the many professionals who may be involved in the care of a young person with bipolar disorder, ranging from the occupational therapist to the child psychiatrist. No matter who you are in this group, you are an important piece in the young person's treatment team. Understanding how this disorder touches his life, and giving him treatment with compassion is paramount.

> "Now I am able to function properly with my right meds and the right doctors who actually care." *Joan*

> "I would have been better off being treated if I had been diagnosed properly. I was miserable as a child, horribly miserable." *Lee*

> "I'm stable now and have been for three years. What a difference." *Jan*

> "I would have been better off properly treated and diagnosed as a child. I don't think I would have felt so alone and different. I always remember feeling like something was wrong, and I didn't know what it was. It sure would have helped an already low self-esteem. I also might have received needed help in school." *Austin*

We applaud those health care professionals who have chosen this very important field of work. We hope that many more will follow their steps and put themselves in a position to do much good. Then, even more professionals will be able to answer the pleas of young people with bipolar disorder by listening to the parents who seek them out for help, by being sensitive to medication side effects that can interfere with a young person's functioning, and by giving both parents and young people the resources they need to learn about this illness. Keeping abreast of the new discoveries and medical advances in treatment, and intervening early before so many years are lost to suffering and misery, will make a huge difference in the lives of the young people they treat. Finally, approaching young people with compassion can touch their hearts and be the difference between success and failure.

What Teachers Can Do

There are so many instances when a teacher did or said something that made a difference for my son. Subtle day-to-day encouragements help him make it through. These teachers do it not because a piece of paper tells them they must, but because they care. One teacher invited my son to become her aide. As a result, his self-esteem was increased, and he was able to demonstrate that he could handle this responsibility.

Another teacher, who suffered from disabilities himself, seemed to know just how to modify my son's work so that he could be successful in his regular education class. He told his students about his own disability, and let my son do the same. This helped to create an atmosphere of acceptance by his peers. Another teacher showed him much compassion and continued to model appropriate behaviors, even when my child's behaviors were less than appropriate. Later we found out that she has a relative with bipolar disorder. Just recently a teacher noted that my son was having a difficult time in the classroom, but she was needed elsewhere and a substitute was taking her place. She showed kindness and understanding by allowing my son to accompany her to the office where she would be working. She also took the time to call me and let me know that a bus ride home that day might be too much.

There are so many examples of ways to help, but they all start with the same key ingredients: understanding and compassion. Children with bipolar disorder are frequently protected under the Individuals with Disabilities Education Act. Through this legislation they may receive accommodations and modifications in the classroom because of their illness. While this is extremely important in bringing a team of teachers together, addressing the child's needs, and keeping everyone on the same page, there is something it can't do. It can never replace the compassion a teacher feels. This compassion may be the difference between carrying out the letter of the law or the intent of the law. It can be the difference between success and failure. (Please see the Epilogue for "My School Day" with and without accommodations.)

> "Mrs.____ would help me when I felt overwhelmed and needed a break." *Alisha, age 7*

> "Teachers need to understand kids get sad too. It is a stressful life for all of us. Be kind and don't yell." *Steven, age 11*

Teachers can answer the plea of young people with bipolar disorder by taking the time to learn about the illness and its manifestation in children, and by becoming an active member of the child's team. Keeping an open line of communication with parents, getting to know your student, and implementing the student's individual accommodations in the classroom are all vital to success in the school setting. Finally, by showing them concern, care and compassion, and building on their individual strengths, you can have a lasting effect on young people with bipolar disorder. Long after you are retired, somewhere, a former student will be remembering the positive influence you had on his life.

What Therapists Can Do

There are a wide variety of therapists with varying backgrounds and degrees. However, what they have in common is a desire to help ease a child's pain. They teach resilience and coping skills to help the child survive whatever difficulties he must face. The personal experiences in this book provide powerful insight into how bipolar disorder feels to the child and how damaging it can be to ignore. Recognizing the biological base of bipolar disorder and the resulting need for intervention and treatment is important.

How can therapists help the young person with bipolar disorder? Therapists are in the unique position of being able to make a difference across several environments and influence all of the people we have discussed thus far. This has the potential of making a large impact in helping the child. Therapists can help parents understand this illness and develop a wide variety of skills as they parent in some of the most difficult circumstances. They can help other health care practitioners by reporting symptoms and observations that could lead to treatment changes. They can also help teachers recognize how the illness impacts children in the classroom and how the implementation of appropriate accommodations can lead to reduced stress and school success.

Teaching the child to recognize moods and what he can and cannot deal with while in those moods is also very helpful. It provides the insight the child needs to make choices and decisions that have positive outcomes. Coping skills are another crucial area for these children. You've read how many turned to maladaptive ways of coping with their illness: substance abuse, promiscuity, risky behavior, anything to quiet the brain. There are healthier alternatives, but they don't come naturally. The therapist can help stock a child's cabinet with a variety of healthy coping skills to weather the storms and even diffuse them before they build beyond control. This insight and these skills become the foundation of a mature emotional capability that allows the child to learn to manage the symptoms of the illness rather than being at the mercy of the illness.

Final Thoughts

When my son looks back on his youth, I never want him to say, "Nobody would help me. Nobody cared. Nobody knew my pain." I would be happy if he said, "Growing up with bipolar disorder was hard, but I had a team of people supporting me. My doctors understood me, listened to me, and took my feelings into consideration to come up with a treatment plan. My teachers made appropriate accommodations that helped me be successful in school. My therapist taught me and those around me how to successfully handle my illness. My parents believed in me, loved me no matter what, were there for me, and always will be."

This is what I want not just for my son but for every young person with bipolar disorder. How does one even begin to accomplish such a goal? It begins with you, the reader. You have been given insight into the intense minds of these young ones. Will you respond? Will you do what you can to support them in their struggles?

This is the gift you can give to future generations. No matter who you are, you can help. Your contribution may be a life dedicated to helping many young people with bipolar disorder, or it may be helping one child. Either way, your contribution is vital. This is not the end. It is the beginning, the beginning of a new era in which understanding and compassion will help erase stigma. This new era starts today. It starts with you. Hear the cries from the past and the pleas for help. Open your heart and extend your hand to help ease the burden carried by young people with bipolar disorder.

EPILOGUE

My School Day without Accommodations

I struggle to open my eyes. Leave me alone. I want to sleep. My body is heavy, my head is swirling. How long has my alarm been ringing? Okay, I'm awake. I sit up in bed, dazed. "Hurry, hurry or you'll be late! Why are you so sleepy?" My nightmare woke me up. I couldn't sleep, I needed to stay awake. I didn't want to dream again. I stumble to my dresser. Where are the socks I like? Not this pair! They never feel right. The top is crooked and they go up too high. I hate the way they feel! No choice. On to breakfast. Who ate my waffles? There is only one left. You know I need two. One is uneven. I NEED two. There aren't two. I won't eat. I'll just brush my teeth. I can't go in the bathroom. It was in my nightmare. The bathroom isn't safe. I can't brush my teeth. It's time to leave. I can't leave. What if my house catches on fire? What if my parents die? I need to stay home. My stomach is churning. I feel sick. Can't I stay home?

The hall is noisy. Kids are pushing. Don't touch me! My sock is crooked. It bothers me. I'm so hungry. First hour, I fall asleep on my desk. The kids laugh when the teacher wakes me up to go to the next class. Am I dreaming again? Is this real? I watch all the kids in class. It's like watching a play. Are they laughing at me again? What are they happy about? It's so hard to smile. Which hour am I in? What is my next class? When does it start? I don't remember. Why can't I remember? What if I go to the wrong class? I better check my schedule. "Don't fidget in class. Pay Attention! You can check your schedule later." I don't listen. I have to know what comes next. Okay, third hour is next. I won't go to the wrong class. Extra work because I didn't pay attention? Not again!

Third hour is test time. I can't concentrate when my sock bothers me. Is my mom okay? I need to call her. I know they won't let me call unless I'm sick. My stomach is rumbling. Can I go to the nurse? Okay, I'll finish my test tomorrow. I call from the nurse's office. Nobody answers. Mom didn't say she was going somewhere today. Did the house catch on fire? Is she okay? My stomach churns. The nurse gives me crackers to settle my stomach. That helps. Go back to class. Finally it's lunch time. What is that smell? I hate the way the lunchroom smells. It's so loud in here. I have one friend. He's absent today. Where will I sit? I find a place in the corner of the room and eat. I hope nobody notices me.

P.E. is next. I love P.E. I run and jump, my body is light and fast now. I'm awake. I'm the BEST basketball player! I can make every shot. Why should I pass you the ball? Sit on the bench? But it wasn't my fault, he was in the way. He shouldn't take the ball from me. That makes me SO MAD! I'm HOT and my sock isn't right! I could redesign this gym. The bleachers don't belong here. Is my mom okay? I remember my dream. I don't want to remember my dream. I have to move or I will die. I run up and down the stairs.

Fifth hour is science. I feel better. Mr. Science is cool. He knows me. He knows I'm smart. I get to do experiments. It keeps my mind busy. He sends me to the office to run an errand. I'm important to him. Maybe the office lady will let me check on my mom. She asks me why I need to call. I can't tell her. It will sound stupid. I tell her I don't remember if I am supposed to ride the bus or be picked up. She believes me. Please answer!

"Mom, are you picking me up today?"

"Of course I am. I told you that this morning. Is everything okay?"

"Yeah, bye!"

Relief! She's okay. Back to science. Only one more class left. I can make it now. Last hour. I sit through math. The teacher is glaring at me. Am I supposed to be doing something? It's my homework. Where is it? I did it. I can't find it in my bag. "Do you want to fail?" She yells at me! I feel stupid. I know I did it. I just can't find it. My stomach churns again. I need to get out of here. The classroom is noisy. My head will explode if I don't leave. Please let me leave. Can I use the bathroom? I really have to go! I walk as slowly as I can to the bathroom. My head feels better. My stomach stops churning. I reach the bathroom. I remember my dream. I can't go in. I wait outside the bathroom as long as I can. I really need to go! I run in and go as fast as I can. My heart is racing, my head is pounding. I'm breathing hard. I did it! School is almost out. I'm going to make it! Hurray! I run out of the bathroom and into Ms. Strict and knock her over. Not Ms. Strict! I didn't mean to. I'm sorry. It doesn't matter. To the Dean's office. In trouble again. I almost made it this time. I'm really sorry.

I'll try again tomorrow. I really try. School is so hard. Won't somebody help me?

My School Day with Accommodations

I struggle to open my eyes. Leave me alone. I want to sleep. My body is heavy, my head is swirling. How long has my alarm been ringing? Okay, I'm awake. I sit up in bed dazed. "Hurry, hurry or you'll be late! Why are you so sleepy?" My nightmare woke me up. I couldn't sleep, I needed to stay awake. I didn't want to dream again. I stumble to my dresser. Where are the socks I like? Not this pair!

They never feel right. The top is crooked and they go up too high. I hate the way they feel! No choice. On to breakfast. Who ate my waffles? There is only one left. You know I need two. One is uneven. I NEED two. There aren't two. I won't eat. I'll just brush my teeth. I can't go in the bathroom. It was in my nightmare. The bathroom isn't safe. I can't brush my teeth. It's time to leave. I can't leave. What if my house catches on fire? What if my parents die? I need to stay home. My stomach is churning. I feel sick. Can't I stay home?

The hall is noisy. Kids are pushing. Don't touch me! My sock is crooked. It bothers me. I'm so hungry. Before first hour, I check in with the nurse, like I always do. I tell her my day didn't start so good. She gives me pretzels to eat. I feel better. But what if I need to call my mom? She reminds me that I can go to Mr. Counselor any time if I get panicked about my parents. Okay. I know I can check on them if I need to. First hour I start to fall asleep on my desk. Ms. Helpful asks me if I can help her with an activity. She knows I'm a good helper. The kids are jealous because they wish they could help too. On to second hour. I watch all the kids in class. It's like watching a play. Are they laughing at me again? What are they happy about? It's so hard to smile. Which hour am I in? What is my next class? When does it start? I don't remember. Why can't I remember? What if I go to the wrong class? Ms. Caring could tell I was getting uncomfortable because I turned over the red card on my desk to give her a secret message. She came over right away. "I can tell you are a little distracted. We are going to work for 10 more minutes on this project and then you can use the last five minutes of class to organize yourself. You will be going to Ms. Write's class next." She winked at me and smiled. I like Ms. Caring. I work really hard for the next 10 minutes.

Third hour is test time. I can't concentrate when my sock bothers me. Is my mom okay? I know I can go to Mr. Counselor if I need to. My stomach starts churning. Ms. Write asks me if I want to take the test in the small, quiet room with Ms. Aide. She writes the answers as I dictate them. She knows it's hard for me to think and write at the same time. I did really well. Finally, it's lunch time. What is that smell? I hate the way the lunchroom smells. It's so loud in here. My best friend is absent today. Where will I sit? Oh, there's Joe. He's my study partner in social skills class. I like him. He wants me to sit with him. I eat my lunch and talk with Joe. He doesn't like the way it smells in here either!

P.E. is next. I love P.E. I run and jump, my body is light and fast now. I'm awake. I'm the BEST basketball player! I can make every shot. Why should I pass you the ball? Oh, the Coach needs me. It's time for a water break? I don't want to leave the game but coach says just for a second to get some water. The water tastes so good and cold. I didn't even know I was thirsty. I take a second drink. I feel much cooler. "Remember, the best players know their teammates and make them work hard too." Yeah. I shouldn't have to make all the shots. It's hard work running up and down the court all hour. Coach says I'm a good player. Then, just for fun, I run up and down all the stairs in the gym. It's a pretty cool gym, but they really should change where the bleachers go.

Fifth hour is science. It's my favorite class. Mr. Science is cool. He knows me. He knows I'm smart. I get to do experiments. It keeps my mind busy. He sends me to the office to run an errand. I'm important to him. I'm still worried about my mom. I stop in Mr. Counselor's office. He wears funny shoes, but he's nice. He lets me call my mom. I hope she's okay. I hope she answers. Please answer!

"Mom, remember you're picking me up today?"

"I remember. Are you in Mr. Counselor's office? Is everything okay?"

"Yeah, bye!"

Relief! She's okay. Back to science. Only one more class left. I can't wait to be out of school. Last hour. I sit through math. The teacher reminds me that my homework is due. Where is it? I did it. I can't find it in my bag. "Don't panic. I'm sure it's in there somewhere!" She helps me look through my bag. There it is! How did it get in my reading folder? The classroom is getting noisy. It's giving me a headache. I feel like my head will explode if I don't leave. I turn over my red card. The teacher sees that the noise is really getting to me. She sends Joe and me together on a bathroom break. We walk slowly to the bathroom. My head feels better. We reach the bathroom. I remember my dream. I don't want to go in but I really have to go. "Are you coming?" asks Joe. "Yeah. In a minute." I wait outside the bathroom as long as I can. I really need to go! I run in and go as fast as I can. My heart is racing, my head is pounding. I'm breathing hard but trying not to let Joe see it. I don't want him to know I'm scared. "Look at that!" says Joe. What is it? Suddenly I forget my dream. Somebody stuffed one of the toilets full of paper towels! What a mess! Joe and I hurry out of the bathroom. We almost knocked Ms. Strict right off her feet. Good thing I wasn't running. We tell Ms. Strict about the bathroom. "Thank you, boys. Will you please go get the janitor for me so we can get this mess cleaned up? I'm so glad you boys caught it when you did."

I check in with the nurse before I go home for the day. How was my day? It was pretty good, but I'm glad school is out! I'll see you tomorrow. Thanks for all the help!

APPENDIX A

Organizations:

Child & Adolescent Bipolar Foundation
1000 Skokie Blvd., Suite 425
Wilmette, IL 60091
Phone: 847-256-8525
Web: www.bpkids.org

The Collaborative Problem Solving Institute
313 Washington St., Suite 402
Newton Corner, MA 02458
Phone: 617-965-3000
Web: www.massgeneral.org/cpsinstitute/

Depressive and Bipolar Support Alliance
730 N Franklin St., Suite 501
Chicago, IL 60610-7224
Phone: 800-826-3632
Web: www.dbsalliance.org

Federation of Families for Children's Mental Health
9605 Medical Center Dr., Suite 280
Rockville, MD 20850
Phone: 240-403-1901
Web: www.ffcmh.org

International Society for Bipolar Disorders
P.O. Box 7168
Pittsburgh, PA 15213-0168
Phone: 412-605-1412
Web: www.isbd.org

Juvenile Bipolar Research Foundation
550 Ridgewood Rd.
Maplewood, NJ 07040
Phone: 866-333-JBRF
Web: www.jbrf.org

The National Alliance on Mental Illness
Colonial Place Three
2107 Wilson Blvd., Suite 300
Arlington, VA 22201-3042
Phone: 888-999-6264
Web: www.nami.org

National Institute of Mental Health
6001 Executive Blvd., Room 8184, MSC 9663
Bethesda, MD 20892-9663
Phone: 866-615-6464
Web: www.nimh.nih.gov

National Mental Health Association
2001 N Beauregard St., 12th Floor
Alexandria, VA 22311
Phone: 800-969-NMHA
Web: www.nmha.org

STARFISH Advocacy Association
3341 Warrensville Center Rd.
Shaker Heights, OH 44122
Web: www.starfishadvocacy.org

More Resources:

The Bipolar Child

www.bipolarchild.com

BPChildren

www.bpchildren.com

Brainstorm: Your Pediatric Bipolar Infosource

www.bpinfo.net

Learning Disabilities Online

www.ldonline.org

School Behavior

www.schoolbehavior.com

Wrightslaw

www.wrightslaw.com

Appendix B

Other works by Tracy Anglada can be found at www.bpchildren.com:

Brandon and the Bipolar Bear: A Story for Children with Bipolar Disorder (also available on DVD)

Turbo Max: A Story for Siblings of Children with Bipolar Disorder

The Student with Bipolar Disorder: An Educator's Guide

Pediatric Bipolar Disorder DVD

Questions Kids Have About Bipolar Disorder (downloadable flyer)

More Recommended Reading for Children:

My Bipolar Roller Coaster Feelings Book by Bryna Hebert

My Roller Coaster Feelings Workbook by Bryna Hebert

Anger Mountain by Bryna Hebert

Darcy Daisy and the Firefly Festival by Lisa Lewandowski, Ph.D., and Shannon M.B. Trost, B.S.

Reading for Adults:

The Bipolar Child, by Demitri F. Papolos, M.D., & Janice Papolos (Broadway; Rev&Expand edition, 2006)

The Bipolar Disorder Survival Guide: What You and Your Family Need to Know, by David J. Miklowitz, Ph.D. (The Guilford Press, 2002)

Bipolar Disorders: A Guide to Helping Children and Adolescents, by Mitzi Waltz (O'Reilly, 2000)

A Brilliant Madness: Living with Manic Depressive Illness, by Patty Duke, Gloria Hochman (Bantam, 1993)

The COBAD Syndrome: New Hope for People Suffering from the Inherited Syndrome of Childhood-Onset Bipolar Disorder with ADHD, by William Niederhut, M. D. (Authorhouse, 2005)

The Explosive Child, by Ross W. Greene, Ph.D. (HarperCollins, 1998)

From Emotions to Advocacy: The Special Education Survival Guide, by Peter W. D. Wright, Pamela Darr Wright (Harbor House Law Press, Inc.; 2nd edition, 2006)

His Bright Light : The Story of Nick Traina, by Danielle Steel (Delta, 2000)

Genius!: Nurturing the Spirit of the Wild, Odd, And Oppositional Child, by George T. Lynn, Joanne Barrie Lynn (Jessica Kingsley Publishers; Revised 2005)

I am Not Sick, I Don't Need Help! by Xavier Amador, Anna-Lica Johanson, Ph.D. (Vida, 2000)

If Your Child Is Bipolar: The Parent-to-Parent Guide to Living with and Loving a Bipolar Child, by Cindy Singer and Sheryl Gurrentz (Perspective Publishing, 2003)

The Life of a Bipolar Child, by Trudy Carlson (Benline Press, 1995)

New Hope for Children and Teens with Bipolar Disorder: Your Friendly, Authoritative Guide to the Latest in Traditional and Complementary Solutions, by Boris Birmaher, M.D. (Three Rivers Press, 2004)

Parenting a Bipolar Child: What to Do and Why, by Gianni Faedda, M.D., and Nancy Austin, PSY.D. (New Harbinger Publications, 2006)

Raising a Moody Child: How to Cope with Depression and Bipolar Disorder, by Mary A. Fristad, Ph.D. and Jill S. Goldberg Arnold, Ph.D. (The Guilford Press, 2004)

Survival Strategies for Parenting Children with Bipolar Disorder, by George T. Lynn (Jessica Kingsley Publishers, 2000)

Straight Talk about Psychiatric Medications for Kids, by Timothy E. Wilens, M.D. Revised edition (The Guilford Press, 2004)

An Unquiet Mind, by Kay Redfield Jamison (Vintage, 1997)

The Ups and Downs of Raising a Bipolar Child: A Survival Guide for Parents, by Judith Lederman and Candida Fink, M.D. (Fireside, 2003)

When Madness Comes Home, by Victoria Secunda (Hyperion, 1998).

Printed in the United States
77450LV00004B/15